LABOR RELATIONS AND PUBLIC POLICY SERIES

REPORT NO. 4

THE NLRB AND SECONDARY BOYCOTTS

by

RALPH M. DERESHINSKY

Published by

INDUSTRIAL RESEARCH UNIT, DEPARTMENT OF INDUSTRY
Wharton School of Finance and Commerce
University of Pennsylvania

Distributed by

University of Pennsylvania Press
Philadelphia, Pennsylvania 19104

Foreword

The federal government's regulation of industrial relations has given rise to important and complex issues of public policy. The Industrial Research Unit of the Wharton School, University of Pennsylvania has encouraged thoughtful consideration of these areas by publishing a series of monographs that trace the development and analyze the implications of these labor policy matters. This report deals with the rules that regulate secondary boycotts as they have been applied and interpreted by the NLRB and the courts.

The public interest is strongly affected by secondary boycotts. Because of the wide variety of situations in which secondary pressure has been utilized and because of the effectiveness of such pressure, the law governing secondary boycotts has become quite complex. Much has been written concerning each problem area, but little has been done to examine all forms of the problem. Mr. Dereshinsky's study undertakes a thorough examination of these issues. In each area, the author studies the historical development and the current application of the law.

Thanks are due to the *Boston University Law Review* for permission to reprint the modified version of a lead article that is contained in Chapter II. Numerous persons also aided the research. The manuscript was typed by Mrs. Veronica M. Kent. John D. Moran, Esq., provided technical assistance. The numerous administrative details were attended to by Mrs. Margaret E. Doyle, Administrative Assistant of the Industrial Research Unit. Kenneth C. McGuiness, Esq., offered valuable advice. The author expresses his thanks to all those who contributed their valuable help. Special thanks are also due to John E. Abodeely, Esq., for his continuing interest, advice, and counsel, and to Mrs. Marie R. Keeney for her fine work in editing the manuscript. The author also is deeply indebted to his family, especially his wife Peggy, for the thoughtfulness and encouragement which they provided. Although many persons aided in this study, the author takes full responsibility for any errors or shortcomings, and for the conclusions herein.

Ralph M. Dereshinsky, Esq., researched and wrote this monograph while a student in the Graduate Division of the Wharton

School, University of Pennsylvania. Prior to earning the Masters in Business Administration degree, he received both his B.A. and J.D. from Boston University. Mr. Dereshinsky is a member of the Massachusetts Bar.

This study was financed by the contributions of the Research Advisory Group of the Industrial Research Unit and by those of the Labor Relations Council of the Wharton School.

HERBERT R. NORTHRUP, *Director*
Industrial Research Unit
Wharton School of Finance and Commerce
University of Pennsylvania

Philadelphia

February 1972

TABLE OF CONTENTS

CHAPTER

CHAPTER I

Introduction

The secondary boycott has been and remains an extremely powerful union tool for exerting economic coercion and for implicating neutral employers, employees, and the public in labor disputes. Secondary boycotts arise out of primary disputes between a *labor union* and a *primary employer*. In the course of the dispute, the union's conduct has the effect and the object of entangling a *secondary neutral employer* in the primary problem by inducing or encouraging his *secondary employees* to cause a cessation of business with the primary employer. The purpose, of course, is to damage economically the secondary employer to such an extent that the primary employer will suffer through loss of customers or through denial of the right of customers to purchase his products. Labor conflicts which extend so far beyond the direct spheres of influence of the primary parties and which spread economic instability and serious disruption obviously affect the public adversely.

The Taft-Hartley Act [1] was the first piece of federal legislation that proscribed secondary boycotts as union unfair labor practices. Prior to 1932, there were no statutory provisions intended to govern labor relations. During this period, the courts relied on the injunction as the means of stopping secondary union activity and of shielding secondary neutral employers. Various state and federal anti-trust laws also provided means by which the judiciary controlled or prohibited secondary activity. [2]

Major legislation during the thirties created a complete change in the law regarding secondary boycotts. The Norris-LaGuardia Act of 1932, [3] enacted during the Hoover Administration, imposed a laissez-faire philosophy upon this area of labor law. The Act removed labor unions from the reach of the anti-trust laws and severely limited the use of the injunction in secondary boycott situations.

---

[1] Taft-Hartley Act, 61 Stat. 136 (1947), *as amended*, 29 U.S.C. §§ 141-44, 151-68 (1964).

[2] *See* H. Northrup and G. Bloom, Government and Labor 13-43 (1963).

[3] 47 Stat. 71 (1932), 29 U.S.C. § 113 (1964).

With a single piece of legislation, Congress thus repealed a century of judicial interpretation and created *laissez faire,* or economic free enterprise, for organized labor as well as for business. Henceforth the Courts were not to interfere with strikes, boycotts, and picketing which were conducted peacefully and otherwise within the law. Moreover, by defining "labor dispute" in a broad fashion, Congress insured labor's right to engage in sympathy strikes, secondary boycotts, stranger picketing, and other activities where nonemployees of a concern come to the aid of a concern's employees in labor disputes directly or by applying pressure upon third parties.[4]

The next significant legislation was the National Labor Relations (Wagner) Act of 1935.[5] Under this New Deal law, collective bargaining became the accepted national labor policy.

The Wagner Act was based upon the philosophy that the failure of employers to accept collective bargaining results in strikes and interferes with the flow of commerce, that the inequality of bargaining power between individual employees and employers who are organized as corporations aggravates depressions by depressing wage rates and reducing purchasing power, and the protection of the right of employees to organize into unions of their own choosing removes most of these difficulties.[6]

The Wagner Act represented an abandonment of laissez-faire policies in labor relations in favor of government support of union growth and collective bargaining. Nevertheless, Congress did not repeal Norris-LaGuardia, and thereby saddled particularly employers with the conflicting philosophy and policies of the Wagner and the Norris-LaGuardia Acts. Under the Wagner Act, Congress proscribed certain employer conduct as unfair labor practices and required employers to bargain collectively with unions chosen by a majority of employees in an appropriate bargaining unit. Abusive union conduct was not similarly prohibited, nor were unions required to bargain in good faith. In addition, because of the Norris-LaGuardia Act, union abuses could not be enjoined.

The passage of the Wagner Act, without any repeal of appropriate Norris-LaGuardia provisions, made secondary boycotts a most powerful weapon. The combined effect of these laws allowed unions to engage in activities that ignored the purpose and

---

[4] H. Northrup and G. Bloom, *supra* note 2, at 24.

[5] National Labor Relations Act (Wagner Act), 49 Stat. 449 (1935), *as amended,* 29 U.S.C. §§ 151-168 (1964).

[6] H. Northrup and G. Bloom, *supra* note 2, at 47.

spirit of the Wagner Act. For example, a union could be rejected as a bargaining agent in a secret ballot vote but then induce a secondary boycott of that company's products because the employer did not grant it exclusive bargaining rights; the employer would violate the Wagner Act if he acceded to the union demand, but the Norris-LaGuardia Act prohibited court relief. Equality of bargaining power was not achieved under the Wagner Act. Instead, the popularity and power of unions were greatly increased. Strong unions were able to utilize the boycott as a means of exerting pressure in order to gain recognition or to gain economic benefits for their members. The Wagner Act made no provision for regulating such activity and the Norris-LaGuardia Act removed the injunction as an effective means of control.

In 1947, Congress acted to restrain some of the abuses that had arisen under the Wagner and Norris-LaGuardia Acts. The Taft-Hartley Amendments created union unfair labor practices which included a ban on secondary boycotts.[7] The pertinent provision, although not specifically mentioning secondary boycotts, was intended effectively to ban such activity. The provisions of Taft-Hartley amended the Norris-LaGuardia Act and now allowed the NLRB to seek an injunction in a Federal District Court as a means of bringing secondary boycotts to a halt. In addition, employers could seek damages in the courts from the union that had conducted a secondary boycott.

The proscriptions on secondary boycotts proved to be less effective than Congress had intended. Several problems arose, attributable in part to the language of section 8(b)(4)(A), that became loopholes in the law. In order to close these loopholes and ban all secondary boycotts, Congress enacted the Landrum-Griffin Amendments of 1959.[8] The new secondary boycott provisions were thereafter in section 8(b)(4)(B). Again, however, the law did not achieve its purpose.

This analysis traces the history of union unfair labor practices arising from secondary boycotts. Each chapter focuses on a particular problem that arose under the Taft-Hartley Act and examines the case law both before and after the 1959 amendments. How effective were the new amendments in closing the

---

[7] Labor Management Relations Act (Taft-Hartley Act), § 8(b)(4)(A), 61 Stat. 141 (1947), *as amended*, 29 U.S.C. § 158(b)(4)(A) (1964).

[8] 29 U.S.C. § 158(b) (1964).

loopholes in the anti-boycott law regarding common situs and ambulatory situs picketing, farmed out work and straight line operations (the "ally doctrine"), consumer picketing, and hot-cargo contract provisions? In order to answer such questions it is necessary to examine not only the statutory provisions and the legislative history of the anti-boycott provisions of the Act, but also to examine the interpretation and application of these laws by the National Labor Relations Board. This analysis is then a study of the administration of secondary boycotts by the National Labor Relations Board and the courts, focusing on how administrative discretion and court review have affected congressional intent and what are some of the practical results therefrom.

CHAPTER II

Common-Situs Picketing

> The gravamen of a secondary boycott is that its sanctions bear, not upon the employer who alone is a party to the dispute, but upon some third party who has no concern in it. Its aim is to compel him to stop business with the employer in the hope that this will induce the employer to give into his employees' demands.[1]

Common-situs picketing, a subject related to the secondary boycott, is a complex area of labor law. As with other secondary boycotts, common-situs picketing involves both a primary employer, with whom the union has a dispute, and a neutral, secondary employer, with whom the union has no dispute. Unlike other secondary-picketing situations, however, both employers share, in some manner, the physical premises that are being picketed. When the two employers occupy the same premises, the problem arises of how to prevent the union from exerting pressure upon the neutral employer while allowing the union to picket that employer with whom it has a dispute. If the union is allowed to picket the premises, the result is that the neutral employer is subjected to pressures from employees with whom he has no direct contact. This may not only prevent the neutral from conducting business with the primary employer, but it may also prevent him from continuing normal business operations with his regular customers. In the alternative, if the union is not allowed to picket the premises, the primary employer, with whom the union may have a legitimate dispute, may escape unscathed due to the inability of the union to effectively apply any pressure.

A union has a right to picket an employer with whom it has a dispute, and the law recognizes as legitimate the union's right to bring pressure to bear upon this employer.[2] The law also

---

Originally published in *Boston University Law Review*, Vol. 50 (Fall 1970). © 1970 by the Trustees of Boston University. Reprinted by permission.

[1] Electrical Workers Local 501 v. NLRB, 181 F.2d 34, 37 (2d Cir. 1950), *aff'd*, 341 U.S. 694 (1951).

[2] Norris-LaGuardia Act § 4, 29 U.S.C. § 104 (1964).

recognizes the right of a neutral employer to be free from the pressure exerted by the union.[3] The conflict between the rights of the neutral and the union is complicated when the primary and secondary employers share the same premises. It is the thesis of this chapter that recent decisions by the National Labor Relations Board (NLRB) have unnecessarily expanded the protection afforded the union to the detriment of the neutral employer.

Prior to 1932, federal statutes and common law provided the bases for the issuance of injunctions to restrain secondary boycotts.[4] The Norris-La Guardia Act,[5] enacted in 1932, made fundamental changes in the legal status of concerted labor activity. One such change made secondary boycotts non-enjoinable [6] provided that the boycott did not impose certain restraints on competition.[7] The National Labor Relations Act,[8] adopted in 1935, further enhanced labor's position with respect to the use of secondary boycotts.[9] That Act expressly guaranteed to employees the right to engage in "concerted activities" for the purpose of

---

[3] Labor-Management Relations Act (Taft-Hartley Act), § 8(b)(4), 29 U.S.C. § 158(b)(4) (1964), *amending* 29 U.S.C. § 158(b)(4) (1958) (*amended by* 73 Stat. 542 (1959)). The relevant portion of § 8 is quoted in note 113 *infra*.
The act does not speak in terms of "picketing" nor does it speak in terms of "secondary" boycott. It has, however, been generally recognized that the intent of the statute is to prohibit only "secondary" boycotts and that picketing is included within that proscription. *See* Koretz, *Federal Regulation of Secondary Strikes and Boycotts—Another Chapter*, 59 Colum. L. Rev. 125 (1959); Lesnick, *The Gravamen of the Secondary Boycott*, 62 Colum. L. Rev. 1363 (1962).

[4] *See* F. Frankfurter and N. Greene, The Labor Injunction 1-46 (1930). The authors trace, in detail, the early history of the labor injunction and the various bases of it in federal and state statutory law and in common law.

[5] 47 Stat. 70 (1932), *as amended*, 29 U.S.C. §§ 101-15 (1964).

[6] 29 U.S.C. § 101 (1964).

[7] *Cf.* United States v. Hutcheson, 312 U.S. 219 (1941), holding that the Clayton Act, Sherman Act and Norris-LaGuardia Act must be read in conjunction with one another in order to determine whether the action alleged to be in violation of the Sherman Act is in reality a "labor dispute" under section 13 of the Norris-LaGuardia Act and thus beyond the equity power of the federal courts. *See also* Nathanson and Wirtz, *The Hutcheson Case: Another View*, 36 Ill. L. Rev. 41 (1941).

[8] 49 Stat. 449 (1935), *as amended*, 29 U.S.C. §§ 151-168 (1964).

[9] National Labor Relations Act §§ 7-8, 49 Stat. 452 (1935), *as amended*, 29 U.S.C. §§ 157-58 (1964).

influencing their employer.[10] As a result of these two acts, the unions were able to increase their power. An essential element of the unions' power was the relatively unrestricted use of the secondary boycott.[11] Recognition of the power inherent in the secondary boycott and its disastrous effect upon neutral employers led, in some part, to the passage of the 1947 amendments to the National Labor Relations Act.[12]

The Taft-Hartley Act proscribed, through specific amendments to the 1935 Act, certain unfair labor practices by employees.[13] One of these provisions dealt with secondary-boycott activity:

> 8(b) It shall be an unfair labor practice for a labor organization or its agents—
>
> . . .
>
> > (4) to engage in, or to induce or encourage the employees of any employer to engage in, a strike or a concerted refusal in the course of their employment to use, manufacture, process, transport, or otherwise handle or work on any goods, articles, materials, or commodities or to perform any services, where an object thereof is:
> >
> > > (A) forcing or requiring any employer or self-employed person to join any labor or employer organization or any employer or other person to cease using, selling, handling, transporting, or otherwise dealing in the products of any other producer, processor, or manufacturer, or to cease doing business with any other person; . . .[14]

This section is phrased in general terms. The activity that is meant to be included within the language "to engage in, or to induce or encourage the employees of any employer" is not clear from the statute, and it is equally unclear what is meant by the proscribed "object" as defined in subsection (A). The ambiguity is not in the nature of the activity that Congress wished to prohibit, but rather is in the lack of any clear distinction between prohibited, secondary activity and protected, primary activity.

---

[10] *Id.* § 7, 49 Stat. 452 (1935), *as amended,* 29 U.S.C. § 157 (1964), provided that employees would have the right to organize, to bargain collectively and to take part in concerted activities for the purpose of collective bargaining.

[11] See remarks of Senator Taft, 93 Cong. Rec. 4198 (1947).

[12] Taft-Hartley Act, 61 Stat. 136 (1947), *as amended,* 29 U.S.C. §§ 141-44, 151-68 (1964).

[13] 61 Stat. 141 (1947), *as amended,* 29 U.S.C. § 158(b) (1964).

[14] Labor Management Relations Act (Taft-Hartley Act) § 8(b)(4)(A), 61 Stat. 141 (1947), *as amended,* 29 U.S.C. § 158(b)(4)(A) (1964).

The lack of any specific standard in section 8(b)(4)(A), therefore, requires that the National Labor Relations Board and the federal courts articulate that distinction.

The legislative history of the Act, as revealed by the remarks of Senator Taft, offers little additional aid to either the Board or the courts.[15]

> [U]nder the provisions of the Norris-La Guardia Act, it became impossible to stop a secondary boycott or any other kind of strike, no matter how unlawful it may have been at common law. All this provision of the bill does is to reverse the effect of the law as to secondary boycotts. . . . So we have so broadened the provisions dealing with secondary boycotts as to make them an unfair labor practice.[16]

As a result, the Board and the courts have approached this problem cautiously, and a body of law has evolved on a case-by-case basis.[17]

THE EMERGENCE OF THE CASE LAW 1949-1959

The early NLRB decisions dealing with common-situs picketing under the Taft-Hartley Act established a policy known as the primary situs rationale. This doctrine afforded neutral parties little protection.

Primary Situs Picketing

Oil Workers Local 346 (Pure Oil Co.)[18] was the first significant case in which the Board considered common-situs picketing under

---

[15] Conference Report of the House of Representatives, H.R. Rep. No. 510, 80th Cong., 1st Sess. 43 (1947). *See also* Hearings on S. 55 and S. J. Res. 22 before the Senate Comm. on Labor and Public Welfare, 80th Cong., 1st Sess. 14, 568, 688, 983, 1614, 1814, 1838 (1947); S. Rep. No. 105, 80th Cong., 1st Sess. Pt. 1, at 3, 22, 54, Pt. 2, at 19 (1947); 93 Cong. Rec. 4844, 4845, 4858 (1947).

[16] 93 Cong. Rec. 4198 (1947).

[17] *See* Koretz, *supra* note 3, at 125-29. *See also* Lesnick, *supra* note 3, for a discussion of the case-by-case approach used by the Board. Note particularly the discussion by Koretz, *supra* note 3, of the reasons why the Congress left the task of final definition to the courts. *See also* Note, *Secondary Boycotts Under Section 8(b)(4)(A) of the Taft-Hartley Act*, 38 Va. L. Rev. 481 (1952).

[18] 84 N.L.R.B. 315 (1949).

the Taft-Hartley Act.[19] Standard Oil, the primary employer, held a lease on dock premises that were used by both Standard Oil and Pure Oil. The union, as a result of a dispute with Standard Oil, established picket lines at Standard's dock and refinery. Since Pure Oil depended upon Standard Oil employees to load its oil, it made an agreement with Standard whereby Pure Oil's employees would handle the shipment of Pure Oil's product for the duration of the strike.[20] Despite this agreement, Pure Oil employees refused to cross the picket lines.[21]

Pure Oil alleged in its complaint that the union had violated section 8(b)(4)(A) by inducing Pure Oil employees to refuse to work on the Standard Oil dock. The Board held that the action of the union was permissible, primary conduct and was not prohibited by section 8(b)(4)(A).[22] The Board held that the activity was primary and lawful because it had occurred at the premises of the primary employer:

> A strike, by its very nature, inconveniences those who do business with the struck employer. Moreover, any accompanying picketing of the employer's premise is necessarily designed to induce and encourage third persons to cease doing business with the picketed employer. It does not follow, however, that such picketing is therefore proscribed by Section 8(b)(4)(A) of the Act.[23]

This rationale—that picketing is permitted if it is confined to the immediate premises of the primary employer—affords no protection to neutral employers who occupy those same premises. The effect of the picketing was not only to prevent Pure Oil from doing business with Standard Oil, but also to prevent Pure Oil from continuing to do business with its own customers and suppliers.[24]

---

[19] 61 Stat. 141 (1947), *as amended*, 29 U.S.C. § 158(b) (1964). See this section as quoted in pertinent part in text accompanying note 14 *supra*.

[20] 84 N.L.R.B. at 316. The agreement between Pure Oil and Standard was reached on June 17, 1948, twenty-one days before the strike against Standard was commenced. *Id.*

[21] *Id.* Pure Oil requested their workers to cross the picket lines on two occasions. On July 8, 1948, the union suggested that the easiest way for Pure Oil to accomplish its objective would be for it to encourage Standard to settle its strike. On July 17, 1948, the union specifically rejected a Pure Oil request that its employees cross the picket lines. *Id.*

[22] *Id.* at 318-19.

[23] *Id.* at 318.

[24] The Board dismissed this argument with the language quoted at note 23 *supra*. It is true that all persons are prevented from doing business with the

A more complex situation was presented the same year in *United Electrical Workers (Ryan Construction Corp.).*[25] In that case the neutral employer, Ryan, had contracted to build an addition to the plant of the primary employer. The site of the construction work and the existing plant were both contained within the same fenced-in area. In order to gain separate access to the construction site, Ryan cut an additional gate in the fence and restricted its use to Ryan's employees. Despite the fact that no employees of the primary employer ever used this gate, when a labor dispute arose between the union and the primary employer, the union picketed all the gates to the plant, including the gate reserved for Ryan personnel. The Ryan employees and suppliers refused to cross the picket lines and an 8(b)(4)(A) complaint against the union was filed.[26]

The Board assumed that an object of picketing the Ryan gate was to pressure the neutral employer to discontinue doing business with the primary, but it nevertheless held that there had been no violation of section 8(b)(4)(A). The decision rested upon the ground that, since the picketing occurred at the premises of the primary employer, it was not secondary activity and was, therefore, not proscribed by the Act.[27] The Board stated that the legislative history of section 8(b)(4)(A) indicated not only that primary activity remained unaffected by that section, but also that the effect of that provision was even more limited:

> It [section 8(b)(4)(A)] was intended only to outlaw certain *secondary* boycotts, whereby unions sought to enlarge the economic battleground beyond the premises of the primary Employer. When

---

primary employer during a strike. It is not always the case, however, that other persons are prevented from conducting their own business with their own customers. *See* Teamsters Local 201 (International Rice Milling Co.), 84 N.L.R.B. 360 (1949), *rev'd*, 183 F.2d 21 (5th Cir. 1950), *rev'd*, 341 U.S. 665 (1951).

[25] 85 N.L.R.B. 417 (1949).

[26] *Id.*

[27] *Id.* at 418. This method of analysis was criticized by the Court of Appeals for the Fifth Circuit in International Rice Milling Co. v. NLRB, 183 F.2d 21 (5th Cir. 1950), *rev'd*, 341 U.S. 665 (1951), *rev'g* 84 N.L.R.B. 360 (1949). The Supreme Court did not decide whether or not the Board's interpretation of the statute was correct. Compare this decision with that of the Court of Appeals for the District of Columbia Circuit in Denver Bldg. Trades Council v. NLRB, 186 F.2d 326 (D.C. Cir. 1950), *rev'd*, 341 U.S. 675 (1951). The Supreme Court in *International Rice* did refer approvingly to the idea that section 8(b)(4)(A) was not intended to affect an ordinary strike, citing *Pure Oil* and *Ryan*. 341 U.S. at 672-73.

picketing is wholly at the premises of the employer with whom the union is engaged in a labor dispute, it cannot be called "secondary" even though, as is virtually always the case, an object of the picketing is to dissuade all persons from entering such premises for business reasons.[28]

The determinative factor was again that the picketing occurred at the premises of the primary employer. If the premises are owned by the primary employer, the picketing is lawful; the objects of the picketing are automatically regarded as incidental to lawful activity; the neutral employer is, therefore, not protected; and the proscription of section 8(b)(4)(A) is not applicable. The rule established by *Ryan Construction Corp.*, like that of *Pure Oil*, was rigid in that it permitted no consideration of the object of the picketing activity.

Board Member Gray, in a vigorous dissent, argued that since the picketing at the separate gate was concededly directed at Ryan,[29] it was secondary activity, and as such, was proscribed by the Act.[30] Member Gray found it an illogical and unsatisfactory result that the majority's holding was based upon geographical proximity rather than upon a sound interpretation of the statute.[31] The dissent argued that the intent of Congress was "to confine labor disputes to the parties immediately involved and to prohibit labor organizations from extending them to other employers neutral in the dispute."[32] If one accepts such an analysis of the intent of the Congress, then clearly the Board cannot analyze a case solely upon the basis of the geographical proximity of the neutral employer to the labor dispute.

The weaknesses of the primary-situs rationale became apparent after the *Ryan* decision.[33] The application of that analysis to

[28] 85 N.L.R.B. at 418 (footnote omitted).

[29] See note 27 *supra* and accompanying text.

[30] 85 N.L.R.B. at 419-20.

[31] *Id.* at 420.

Nowhere in the legislative reports or debates, as far as I have been able to discover, has Congress indicated that this protection to neutral employers should be lost simply because of the geographical proximity of the situs of the neutral employer's enterprise to that of the struck plant. *Id.*

[32] *Id.*

[33] Several cases, however, continued to follow the primary-situs rationale. *See* Lesnick, *supra* note 3, at 1367 n.16. *See* Koretz, *supra* note 3, at 136-41;

fact patterns similar to those of *Ryan* manifested the logical defi-
ciencies of that doctrine.[34] It became apparent that there could
never be a violation under 8(b)(4)(A) if the two employers occupied the same premises.[35] Despite the existence of a statute
that was intended to provide protection for the neutral employer,
there was, in fact, no protection afforded under these circumstances. It should be noted at this point that the dissent in *Ryan*
considered factors that were later deemed necessary to the analysis of common-situs problems.[36]

Ambulatory-Situs Picketing

The demise of the primary-situs doctrine paralleled the development of a more sensitive analysis in a number of related cases in
which the issue was the converse of that presented in *Pure Oil*
and *Ryan*: rather than the union picketing at premises of the
primary employer, the union picketed at premises of the neutral
employer. The unions defended the picketing on the ground that
employees of the primary employer were present on the neutral
employer's premises. Although under the geographical test of
Pure Oil and *Ryan* the picketing would be secondary action and
therefore prohibited, the Board recognized as legitimate the union's right to publicize its demands.

The Board considered the effect of section 8(b)(4)(A) upon
picketing at the premises of the neutral employer [37] in the *Team-*

Note, *Common Situs Rules Fade Away as NLRB and Courts Look to Object
of Union's Picketing in Taft-Hartley Section 8(b)(4)(A) Cases*, 45 Geo.
L. J. 614 (1957).

[34] See cases cited note 27 *supra*.

[35] This proposition is suggested by the language of the court in International
Rice Milling v. NLRB, 183 F.2d 21 (5th Cir. 1950), *rev'd*, 341 U.S. 665
(1951), *rev'g* 84 N.L.R.B. 360 (1949).

> To allow the Board to rule such activity as prohibited by the statute
> not to be a violation thereof, simply because it occurred in the vicinity
> of the struck employer's plant, would render the section ineffective and
> insufficient.

Id. at 27.

[36] Member Grey relied upon the "necessary affect" of the picketing to draw
the conclusion that the picketing was secondary and thus violative of section
8(b)(4)(A). In so doing he evaluated the object of the picketing and concluded that it was directed against Ryan and not against the primary
employer. In addition, Member Grey relied upon an interpretation of the
statute different from that of the majority. 85 N.L.R.B. at 419.

[37] The Board had found a violation of § 8(b)(4)(A) in a few instances prior
to *Pure Oil* and the articulation of the primary-secondary dichotomy. *See*

sters Local 807 (Schultz Refrigerated Service, Inc.)[38] case. On August 28, 1948, Schultz Refrigerated Service triggered a labor dispute when it moved its truck terminal from New York City to New Jersey and thereafter refused to renegotiate a contract with the union that had represented its employees. Since Schultz continued to service the same customers in and around the New York area, the union picketed the Schultz trucks as they made deliveries. In addition, since Schultz no longer had business premises within New York City, the picketing was always conducted at the premises of neutral employers. The pickets carried signs that clearly stated that the dispute was with Schultz alone. Further, the pickets were on the premises of the neutral employer only when the Schultz trucks were present.[39]

A divided Board held that this picketing did not constitute secondary activity and, therefore, that it was not prohibited by section 8(b)(4)(A).[40] The majority reasoned that since there was no "primary situs" of the dispute in New York City, picketing the trucks at the premises of neutral employers was the only effective means of applying pressure to Schultz.[41] The dissent rejected this reasoning and argued that there was "no mandate [within the Act] to guarantee a labor organization the right to conduct an effective strike . . . ."[42] The dissent also argued that the special problem presented by the lack of any primary premises within the city did not require a special solution.[43] Although it is true that the Act does not guarantee to a labor union that

---

Denver Bldg. Trades Council, 82 N.L.R.B. 1195 (1949), *rev'd*, 186 F.2d 326 (D.C. Cir. 1950), *rev'd*, 341 U.S. 675 (1951); Electrical Workers Local 501, 82 N.L.R.B. 1028 (1949), *enforced*, 181 F.2d 34 (2d Cir. 1950), *aff'd*, 341 U.S. 694 (1951); United Bhd. of Carpenters, 81 N.L.R.B. 802 (1949), 184 F.2d 60 (10th Cir. 1950), *cert. denied*, 341 U.S. 947 (1951).

[38] 87 N.L.R.B. 502 (1949).

[39] *Id.* at 503.

[40] *Id.* at 508-09.

[41] The majority suggested, but did not rely upon, an alternative rationale for holding that the picketing did not violate section 8(b)(4)(A). It could be argued that the Schultz trucks were the premises of the primary employer in New York City and thus that the picketing of the premises of the primary employer was permissible. See *id.* at 507 n.13. The Board chose, however, to base its opinion upon its conclusion that the trucks were the "most appropriate objects of primary pressure." *Id.* at 507.

[42] *Id.* at 512-13.

[43] *Id.* at 512.

it will be able to apply pressure effectively to the primary employer, it can be inferred from the congressional action that created dual rights in both the neutral employer and the union that the Board must develop an analysis that allows for a balancing of the interests of both.[44]

In the *Schultz* case, the majority decision established several safeguards for the protection of neutral third parties. In resolving the problem in this manner, the Board in *Schultz* proceeded beyond the "geographic location of the dispute" rationale and, for the first time, examined the object of the picketing.[45] In so doing, the Board sought to protect the interests of the union by recognizing that picketing at a roving situs was the only effective means of publicizing the dispute. At the same time, however, the interests of the neutral employers were at least partially protected by limiting the right of the union to picket to the times when, and the locations where, Schultz trucks were present. Further, the Board noted that the union's picket signs stated that the dispute was with Schultz alone, thus affording additional protection to the neutral employer.[46]

The safeguards that were outlined in the *Schultz* case were more clearly defined in *Sailors' Union (Moore Dry Dock Co.)*.[47] The union in this case was involved in a labor dispute with the owners of the ship *Phopho*. Since the ship was in dry dock undergoing alterations, and since the owner of the premises, Moore Dry Dock Co., would not allow the union's pickets within its gates, the union established its picket line at the gates of that neutral employer. The pickets carried placards that read "S.S. *Phopho* unfair to the Sailors' Union of the Pacific, A.F.L." [48] As a result of the picketing, all Moore employees refused to work on the *Phopho* although they continued to work on all other projects at the dry dock.

---

[44] See notes 2 and 3 *supra* and accompanying text. It has already been suggested that the law recognizes the rights of both the union and the neutral employer. It is thus conceded that the Act does not guarantee either party's rights. This does not mean, however, that the Act prohibits the Board from developing standards by which to alleviate the tension between the two parties. In this sense, unique factual situations do require that the Board develop "special solutions."

[45] See note 33 *supra*.

[46] 87 N.L.R.B. at 503.

[47] 92 N.L.R.B. 547 (1950).

[48] *Id.* at 561.

Moore Dry Dock Company filed a complaint with the NLRB, alleging that the union picket line was in violation of section 8(b)(4)(A).[49] The Board, citing *Schultz, Ryan* and *Pure Oil,* commenced its analysis with the proposition that section 8(b)(4) (A) was designed to prohibit secondary activity and was not intended to affect primary activity. Since permissible, primary activity often has incidental secondary effects, the Board reasoned that the object of the picketing did not provide a workable criterion.[50] The Board chose instead to rely upon the primary-situs standard that it had developed in *Pure Oil, Ryan* and *Schultz.*[51] Since, by this standard, picketing at the "primary situs" of the labor dispute is primary activity, the Board had to determine whether or not the Moore shipyard was the primary situs of the labor dispute. Analogizing this situation to that presented in *Schultz*, the Board held that the *Phopho* was the ambulatory situs of the labor dispute and, therefore, the activity was not secondary within the *Pure Oil* test.[52] At this point the Board asked the additional question of whether or not the union should be allowed to picket in front of the neutral employer's gates in order to publicize its dispute with the primary employer. In answer to this question the Board developed a set of standards to be applied to situations that exist "[w]hen a secondary employer is harboring the *situs* of a dispute between a union and a primary employer."[53]

> In the kind of situation that exists in this case, we believe that picketing of the premises of a secondary employer is primary if it

---

[49] *Id.* at 556-57.

[50] The majority reasoned:

[I]f Samsoc, the owner of the S. S. *Phopho,* had had a dock of its own in California to which the *Phopho* had been tied up while undergoing conversion by Moore Dry Dock employees, picketing by the Respondent at the dock site would unquestionably have constituted *primary* action, *even though* the Respondent might have expected that the picketing would be more effective in persuading Moore employees not to work on the ship than to persuade the seamen aboard the *Phopho* to quit that vessel. The difficulty in the present case arises therefore, not because of any difference in picketing objectives, but from the fact that the *Phopho* was not tied up at its own dock . . . .

Id. at 548 (footnote omitted) (emphasis added).

[51] *Id.* at 549. See discussion in text accompanying note 18 *supra.*

[52] 92 N.L.R.B. at 549.

[53] *Id.*

meets the folloying conditions: (a) The picketing is strictly limited
to times when the *situs* of dispute is located on the secondary employer's premises; (b) at the time of the picketing the primary
employer is engaged in its normal business at the *situs;* (c) the
picketing is limited to places reasonably close to the location of the
situs; and (d) the picketing discloses clearly that the dispute is
with the primary employer.[54]

Necessary pre-conditions to these standards are that there be a
primary, roving situs and that the situs be located upon the premises of a neutral employer.[55] The standards delineated in (a) and
(b) protect the union's right to apply pressure to the primary
employer. At the same time the standards set down in (c) and
(d) restrict the scope of the picketing, and thus limit the harm
suffered by the neutral employer to that ordinarily incidental to
primary activity.

The Board in *Moore* attempted to balance the conflicting rights
of the union and the neutral employer.

> When the *situs* is ambulatory, it may come to rest temporarily at
> the premises of another employer. . . . Essentially the problem is
> one of balancing the right of a union to picket at the site of its
> dispute as against the right of a secondary employer to be free
> from picketing . . . .[56]

The Board, by harmonizing these conflicting interests, in fact
developed a separate standard for the ambulatory-situs situation.
The balancing-of-interests test was not immediately applied to the
situation where the neutral employer was working on the premises of the primary employer. Rather, in those situations, the
Board continued to apply the *Pure Oil* and *Ryan* test—whether or
not the premises being picketed were those of the primary employer.[57]

The eventual application of the *Moore* standards to the *Pure
Oil* and *Ryan* situation was foreshadowed in *Denver Building*

---

[54] *Id.* (footnotes omitted).

[55] The Schultz test would appear to require that the case involve a roving
situs, because otherwise the union could picket at the premises of the primary employer.

[56] 92 N.L.R.B. at 549.

[57] Teamsters Local 249 (Crump, Inc.), 112 N.L.R.B. 311 (1955); *cf.* Los
Angeles Building Trades Council (Standard Oil of Cal.), 105 N.L.R.B. 868
(1953); H. N. Thayer Co., 99 N.L.R.B. 1122 (1952), *modified,* 213 F.2d 748
(1st Cir. 1953), *cert. denied,* 348 U.S. 883 (1954).

Trades Council.[58] That case involved the picketing of a construction site at which all but one of the subcontractors were members of unions affiliated with the Denver Building and Construction Trades Council. The union argued that the picketing was directed only at the non-union subcontractor, despite the fact that it necessarily affected the general contractor. The Board held that the relationship between a general contractor and a subcontractor in the construction industry was one of "doing business" [59] and, therefore, the picketing was in violation of section 8(b)(4)(A). Since the subcontractor and general contractor were independent of each other and since a necessary object of the picketing was to influence the general contractor to breach his contract with the subcontractor, the Board held that the primary-situs doctrine did not apply.

The Court of Appeals for the District of Columbia Circuit reversed the Board on the basis of the primary-situs standard.[60] The court reasoned that since the general contractor had made a contract with the subcontractor that resulted in the employment of the non-union employees, he was not neutral to the dispute. The effect of this analysis was that the primary-situs standard did apply and the picketing was held permissible.[61]

The Supreme Court reversed the lower court's decision and affirmed the decision of the Board.[62] The Court first considered the relationship between the subcontractor and the general contractor.

> The fact that the contractor and subcontractor were engaged on the same construction project, and that the contractor had some supervision over the subcontractor's work, did not eliminate the status of each as an independent contractor, or make the employees of one the employees of the other. The business relationship between independent contractors is too well established in the law to be overriden without clear language doing so.[63]

---

[58] 82 N.L.R.B. 1195 (1949), *rev'd*, 186 F.2d 326 (D.C. Cir. 1950), *rev'd*, 341 U.S. 675 (1951).

[59] *Id.* at 1196.

[60] Denver Bldg. Trades Council v. NLRB, 186 F.2d 326 (D.C. Cir. 1950), *rev'd*, 341 U.S. 675 (1951).

[61] *Id.*

[62] NLRB v. Denver Bldg. Trades Council, 341 U.S. 675 (1950).

[63] *Id.* at 689-90.

In so ruling the Court eliminated the primary-situs doctrine from application to the case. The general contractor in fact was a neutral employer, and since the neutral employer owned or controlled the premises, the union could not defend its action on the basis of the analysis used in *Pure Oil* and *Ryan*. Thus, the Court in *Denver* subjected the construction industry to the same regulation that would later be applied to all common-situs problems.

More significantly, the Supreme Court recognized that common-situs problems should be decided in accordance "with the dual congressional objectives of preserving the right of labor organizations to bring pressure to bear on offending employers in primary labor disputes and of shielding unoffending employers and others from pressures in controversies not their own." [64] By analyzing the relationship between the two employers rather than relying upon a geographical test, the Board and the Court balanced the interests of the parties. Since an object of the union's picketing was to force the neutral to cease doing business with the primary, the picketing violated section 8(b)(4)(A).

Demise of the Primary-Situs Rationale

The demise of the primary-situs rationale became complete when the Board applied the *Moore* standards to a non-ambulatory-situs situation in *Local 55, United Carpenters (Professional & Business Men's Life Ins. Co.)*.[65] In this case Professional & Business Men's Life, the general contractor, employed both union and non-union workers on a construction project. A union sought to have Professional & Business Men's Life recognize it as the bargaining agent for the non-union employees. When Professional & Business Men's Life refused to recognize the union, a picket line was established at the construction site. As a result of the picketing, the employees of two unionized subcontractors refused to continue their work at the site. The Board did not attempt to use the primary-situs rationale of *Pure Oil* and *Ryan,* but rather applied one of the *Moore* standards to the non-ambulatory common-situs situation.

> [T]he fact that the picketing takes place at the situs of the primary employer's regular place of business rather than at an ambulatory situs is not controlling; in both situations, picketing at a common

---

[64] *Id.* at 692.

[65] 108 N.L.R.B. 363, *enforced,* 218 F.2d 226 (10th Cir. 1954).

situs is unlawful if the picketing sign fails to disclose that the dispute is confined to the primary employer.[66]

Despite a statement by the Board that this was not the end of the primary-situs doctrine,[67] and despite the lack of any mention of the *Moore* case, the Board did apply one of the *Moore* standards to a non-ambulatory, common-situs situation. Although the Board did not specifically adopt the *Moore* balancing test, it did recognize the affirmative duty of the union at the common situs to respect the interests of the neutral employer.

The effect of the holding in *Professional & Business Men's Life* was to afford greater protection to the neutral employer at a common situs by restricting, but not denying, the union's right to picket the premises. As a result of the decision, the union was required to conform to the provisions of the Act, even when picketing at the premises of the primary employer. The Court of Appeals for the Tenth Circuit, in affirming the decision of the Board,[68] applied the *Moore* standards to the non-ambulatory common-situs situation.[69]

> To reconcile these conflicting interests, the Board in Sailors' Union of the Pacific . . . evolved criteria for determining when picketing at a common situs would be considered legitimate primary picketing or unlawful secondary picketing . . . .[70]

The court specifically adopted the four criteria of *Moore* and applied them to *Professional & Business Men's Life*.[71] The court then held that the Board was correct in finding that the picket signs were directed at the secondary employers and, therefore, that the picketing was prohibited by the Act. This result conflicted sharply with both *Pure Oil* and *Ryan,* where the Board had assumed that the object of the strikes was to apply pressure to secondary employers and, yet, had held the activity permissible.[72]

Subsequently, in *Retail Clerks Local 1017 (Crystal Palace Market),*[73] the Board specifically extended the *Moore* standards to

---

[66] *Id.* at 366.

[67] *Id.* at 370.

[68] NLRB v. Local 55, United Carpenters, 218 F.2d 226 (10th Cir. 1954).

[69] *Id.* at 231.

[70] *Id.*

[71] *Id.*

[72] See note 18 *supra* and accompanying discussion.

[73] 116 N.L.R.B. 856 (1956), *enforced,* 249 F.2d 59 (9th Cir. 1957).

control non-ambulatory common-situs picketing. As a result, the *Moore* standards became the sole criteria for determining the legality of all common-situs picketing—ambulatory and non-ambulatory.

A brief review of the development of these standards manifests the gradual emergence of a concern for the interests of *both* the union *and* the neutral employer. In *Schultz* the Board had distinguished the ambulatory-situs situation from the *Pure Oil* and *Ryan* situations. The Board in *Moore* developed a method of analysis by which to balance the interests of the union and the neutral employer. An increased awareness on the part of the Board and the courts that equitable enforcement of the Act required the recognition of the dual congressional objectives of protecting the conflicting interests of the unions and the neutral employers led inevitably to the demise of the primary-situs rationale.

MODIFICATION OF THE EXISTING STANDARDS

The evolution of the standards governing common-situs picketing, however, was not accomplished with the application of the *Moore* standards to all the common-situs situations. As unique situations arose it was necessary to modify the *Moore* standards themselves to achieve the objectives of Congress in passing section 8(b)(4)(A).

Modification of the Moore Doctrine

The *Brewery Drivers Local 67 (Washington Coca-Cola Bottling Works, Inc.)*[74] case presented one such novel situation. The union representing Washington's truck drivers was engaged in a strike against Washington Coca-Cola Bottling Works. Pickets were placed at the plant of the primary employer in downtown Washington. Subsequently, pickets followed the delivery trucks to the retail outlets in order to picket them while they took orders and made deliveries. The pickets were not withdrawn from the retail outlets until the retailers agreed not to purchase from Washington Coca-Cola. The Board had "no difficulty"[75] finding that the object of this picketing was to affect the retail outlets by inducing

---

[74] 107 N.L.R.B. 299 (1953), *aff'd*, 220 F.2d 380 (D.C. Cir. 1955).

[75] *Id.* at 302.

the customers and suppliers of the neutrals to refuse to do business with them.[76]

In defense of its actions, the union relied upon *Schultz* and *Moore*.[77] The Board, however, distinguished those cases upon the fact that in both *Schultz* and *Moore* there had been no permanent, primary premises that could be picketed effectively.[78] The Court of Appeals for the District of Columbia Circuit, in enforcing the Board's order, held that "since Coca-Cola had a permanent place of business that could be and was picketed, the 'ambulatory situs' doctrine did not apply."[79] The picketing of the retail outlets was held to be an illegal, secondary boycott.

The Board based its holding upon the particular facts involved. Since primary employees were at the plant at least four times a day, and since the plant was located in downtown Washington, D.C., the union could have publicized its dispute and exerted pressure upon the primary employer at the primary situs.[80] In so holding the Board revived that part of the *Schultz* holding that was based upon the lack of any real opportunity for the union to exert pressure effectively without the use of ambulatory picketing.[81] *Washington Coca-Cola* created an exception to the ambulatory-situs doctrine such that if the primary employer could be picketed "effectively" at the primary employer's premises, then picketing at a neutral employer's premises would be a violation of section 8(b)(4)(A). Although the Board added a pre-condition to the *Moore* standards, the result was consistent with the policy of balancing the conflicting interests of the union and the neutral employer.

---

[76] *Id.*

[77] The union's defense was based upon the arguments that the trucks were the situs of the dispute; that this situs was ambulatory; and thus that they had a right to picket the trucks wherever the trucks went. See note 38 *supra* and accompanying text.

[78] 107 N.L.R.B. at 303.

[79] Brewery Drivers Local 67 v. NLRB, 220 F.2d 380, 381 (D.C. Cir. 1955). (The court affirmed the Board's order on the basis it was supported by substantial evidence. The court did set forth the issue as quoted in the text.)

[80] 107 N.L.R.B. at 303.

[81] *Compare* Teamsters Local 807 (Schultz Refrigerated Serv., Inc.), 87 N.L.R.B. 502 (1949), *with* Sailors' Union (Moore Dry Dock), 92 N.L.R.B. 547 (1950).

Several cases that were decided subsequent to *Washington* dealt with this exception to the ambulatory-situs doctrine.[82] For example, the Board, in *Painters Local 193 (Pittsburgh Plate Glass Co.)*[83] held that the *Washington* doctrine did not bar the application of the *Moore* standards where the union could not have picketed the premises of the primary employer effectively. The Board examined the question of the effectiveness of the opportunity to picket the primary employer in terms of both the union's right to exert pressure on the primary employer and the union's right to publicize the dispute. Since in *Pittsburgh Plate* the primary employer's employees were seldom at the plant, and since the plant was in a remote section of town,[84] the Board held that the union could not have picketed effectively if its pickets had been limited to the premises of the primary employer. The Board did, however, find a violation of section 8(b)(4)(A) because the union had failed to observe one of the *Moore* standards.[85] The rule to be drawn from this case would appear to be that the *Washington* doctrine is a pre-condition to the application of the *Moore* standards.

The Board in *General Drivers Local 968 (Otis Massey Co.)*[86] used a method of analysis that clarifies the close interrelationship between the *Washington* doctrine and the *Moore* standards. *Otis Massey* involved a dispute between the primary employer and its truck drivers and warehousemen. The union picketed the warehouse as well as various construction sites where the primary employer was performing subcontracts. The Board did not consider the application of the *Washington* doctrine; rather, the Board

---

[82] *See* Teamsters Local 657 (Southwestern Motor Transp., Inc.), 115 N.L.R.B. 981 (1956); Seattle Carpenters Council (Cisco Constr. Co.), 114 N.L.R.B. 27 (1955); Teamsters Local 612 (Goodyear Tire & Rubber Co.), 112 N.L.R.B. 30 (1955); Sales Drivers Local 859 (Campbell Coal Co.), 110 N.L.R.B. 2192 (1954), *enforcement denied*, 229 F.2d 514 (D.C. Cir. 1955), *cert. denied*, 351 U.S. 972 (1956).

[83] 110 N.L.R.B. 455 (1954).

[84] The Board specifically found that the employees were at the plant only twice a day and then only to report for work and to check out. Sometimes the employees did not even do that. *Id.* at 457. The Board also found that the plant was located in the industrial section, two and one half miles from the center of town. *Id.*

[85] *Id.* at 456. The Board found that the union did not identify the primary employer with sufficient specificity and thus violated the fourth Moore standard. See decision quoted at note 54 *supra*.

[86] 109 N.L.R.B. 275 (1954), *enforcement denied*, 225 F.2d 205 (5th Cir. 1955), *cert. denied*, 350 U.S. 914 (1955).

held that the union did not meet the first *Moore* standard because the secondary employers were not "harboring" the situs of the dispute.[87] It is difficult to distinguish between the facts in *Otis Massey* and *Pittsburgh Plate*. The two cases appear to involve the same analytical considerations. It is difficult, therefore, to understand why the *Washington* doctrine was not even discussed in the *Otis Massey* case. The answer is, perhaps, that the *Washington* doctrine does not come into effect until there is ambulatory situs and until the ambulatory situs comes to rest on the premises of a neutral employer. This is, in reality, the "necessary pre-condition" to the *Moore* standards discussed above.[88] *Otis Massey* clarifies the relationship between *Washington* and *Moore* by emphasizing that once it appears that there is an ambulatory situs, then the *Washington* doctrine is applicable. The *Washington* doctrine is, therefore, an additional factor, to be considered prior to the application of the *Moore* standard.

Confusion as to the exact application of the *Washington* doctrine also existed in the courts. Although the Court of Appeals for the District of Columbia Circuit had affirmed the Board's decision in *Washington,* it criticized that same doctrine in *Sales Drivers Local 859 v. NLRB (Campbell Coal Co.).*[89] The Board had found that the truck drivers involved in the dispute spent twenty-five percent of each working day at the premises of the primary employer, twenty-five percent en route to the construction site, and fifty percent at the construction site. The Board, relying upon *Washington,* held that the union had an effective means of picketing the primary employer at his plant.[90] The court reversed this holding and remanded the case to the Board.[91] The court labeled the *Washington* doctrine a "rigid rule" and held that the existence of a permanent place of business that can be picketed effectively was a factor to be considered, but should not be conclusive in determining whether or not the picketing was permissible.[92] On remand,

---

[87] *Id.*

[88] *Id.* at 278. This standard requires that the picketing be strictly limited to those times when the situs of the dispute is located on the neutral employer's premises.

[89] 229 F.2d 514 (D.C. Cir. 1955), *cert. denied,* 351 U.S. 972 (1956).

[90] Sales Drivers Local 859, 110 N.L.R.B. 2192, 2194 (1954), *enforcement denied,* 229 F.2d 514 (D.C. Cir. 1955), *cert. denied,* 351 U.S. 972 (1956).

[91] 229 F.2d at 514.

[92] *Id.* at 517.

the Board held that there had been several violations of the *Moore* standards "including, but not limited to, the fact that the Respondent could have effectively picketed Campbell Coal at its own business premises . . . ." [93]

It is submitted that the final decision of the Board demonstrates the flexibility of the *Washington* doctrine. From the date of the passage of the Taft-Hartley Act in 1947, it has been clear that the interests of the union and the neutral employers conflict sharply. The need to balance these conflicting interests led to the development of the *Moore* standards. The *Washington* doctrine, by affording the union the right to publicize its dispute effectively and to apply pressure to the primary employer, when able to do so without unnecessarily enmeshing neutral employers, increases the flexibility of the balancing test. *Campbell Coal* has not been followed by the Board nor by most of the circuit courts; rather, the *Washington* doctrine has been applied, so that if the primary employer has a permanent place of business that can be picketed effectively, the ambulatory-situs doctrine will not be applicable. [94]

Perhaps the clearest statement of the *Washington* doctrine is found in *Local 657, Teamsters (Southwestern Motor Transport, Inc.)*. [95] The union in this case was engaged in a dispute for recognition with the primary employer, Southwestern. After picketing the primary employer's premises for several weeks, the union pickets followed Southwestern's trucks to neutral employers' premises. The facts found by the Board indicate that the union's activity would have conformed to the *Moore* standards. [96] The Board, however, held that since all the drivers had to cross the picket lines at the premises of the primary employer twice a day, the *Washing-*

---

[93] Sales Drivers Local 859 (Campbell Coal Co.), 116 N.L.R.B. 1020, 1022-23 (1956), *enforced sub nom.* Truck Drivers Local 728 v. NLRB, 249 F.2d 512 (D.C. Cir. 1957), *cert. denied,* 355 U.S. 958 (1958).

[94] Commission House Drivers Local 400 (Euclid Foods, Inc.), 118 N.L.R.B. 130 (1957); Local 117, United Glass Workers (Mason and Dixon Lines, Inc.), 117 N.L.R.B. 622 (1957); United Steelworkers (Barry Controls, Inc.), 116 N.L.R.B. 1470 (1956), *enforced,* 250 F.2d 184 (1st Cir. 1957).

[95] 115 N.L.R.B. 981 (1956).

[96] The Board found that the union picketed the trucks at the premises of neutral employers only when the trucks were at those premises. The picket lines were established as near as possible to the trucks. The picket signs were specifically directed at the employees of the primary employer. Since the dispute involved the truck drivers, it was unquestioned that the trucks were the situs of the dispute. Finally, the primary employer was found to be engaged in his normal business at the premises of the neutral employer. *Id.* at 982.

ton doctrine applied and, therefore, the union's activity violated section 8(b) (4) (A).[97]

> The Board has, however, continued to recognize this exception [the roving-situs doctrine] for what it is, and has therefore declined to apply it when the reason for its application—the inability of the union to put pressure on the primary employer through his own employees at his place of business—does not exist. This conclusion rests on the sound premise that a union which can direct its inducements to the primary employer's employees at the primary employer's premises, does not seek to accomplish any more with respect to those same employees by directing the same inducements to those same employees at the premises of some other employer. Consequently, the only reasonable inference in such a situation is that inducements which are ostensibly directed at the primary employer's employees are in fact directed at the employees of the secondary employers. In concluding, therefore, that picketing under such circumstances violates Section 8(b) (4) (A) and (B) of the Act, the Board is effectuating the congressional objective of shielding unoffending employers from pressures and controversies not their own, while at the same time leaving the union free to exert its pressures on the primary employer in a manner which will, at the most, have only an incidental effect on the secondary employers.[98]

Thus, despite the *Campbell* case, the *Washington* doctrine remained viable. The *Washington* doctrine and the *Moore* standards set the requirements for determining whether ambulatory-situs picketing violates section 8(b) (4) (A). With the demise of the primary-situs rationale in *Professional & Business Men's Life Insurance*[99] and *Crystal Palace*,[100] the *Moore* standards had also become the requirements for non-ambulatory common-situs picketing. The policy set forth in *Southwestern Motor Transport*—to "minimize its [picketing's] impact on neutral employees insofar as this can be done without substantial impairment of the effectiveness of the picketing in reaching the primary employees"[101]—was consistent with the policy underlying the formulation of the *Moore* standards and their subsequent application to non-ambulatory common-situs situations.

---

[97] *Id.*

[98] *Id.* at 983-84 (footnotes omitted).

[99] 108 N.L.R.B. 363, *enforced*, 218 F.2d 226 (10th Cir. 1954). See note 65 *supra* and accompanying text.

[100] 116 N.L.R.B. 856 (1956), *enforced*, 249 F.2d 591 (9th Cir. 1957). See note 73 *supra* and accompanying text.

[101] *Id.* at 859.

Misapplication of Moore

Shortly after the *Moore* standards became applicable to all common-situs picketing, several cases stimulated a re-examination of the application and interpretation of certain of those standards. In *Local 618, Automotive Employees (Incorporated Oil Co.)*,[102] the union was engaged in a labor dispute with a gasoline service-station chain. In furtherance of the strike, the union picketed the company's retail gasoline stations. A picketline was established at one station that was being rebuilt, while business continued from temporary facilities on the premises. The construction workers, who were employed by a neutral employer, refused to cross the picket lines. The primary employer discontinued operations at this site and removed all his employees and all the company signs. The union then stopped picketing. Shortly thereafter, only the construction work was resumed. Despite the absence of the primary employees, the union again picketed this station. The pickets were successful and the construction work was again brought to a halt.[103]
Applying the *Moore* standards to this case, the Board held that since no primary employees were present, there was no question that the picketing was aimed at secondary employees.

> . . . The essential issue of this case is not altered by the fact that [the primary employer] owned the Manchester location and intended, at a future date, once again to conduct its retail gasoline business there. Title to property of itself cannot be the determinative factor in assessing the legality under this statute of picketing activities.[104]

The *Moore* standards require that the primary employer be engaged in normal operations at the site being picketed.[105] Since this condition had not been met, the union had violated section 8(b) (4) (A).

The Court of Appeals for the Eighth Circuit reversed the Board's decision and held that the picketing was primary because it was a continuation of the picketing that had begun before the construction work was started and before the primary employees were

----

[102] 116 N.L.R.B. 1844 (1956), *enforcement denied*, 249 F.2d 332 (8th Cir. 1957).

[103] *Id.* at 1845.

[104] *Id.* at 1848.

[105] See note 47 *supra* and accompanying text.

removed from the Manchester location.[106] The only precedent that supplies any justification for overturning the Board's decision was the primary-situs rationale.[107] Prior cases under the *Moore* standard balanced the rights of the union—to exert pressure and to publicize its dispute—with the interests of the neutral employers —to be free from labor disputes in which they are not primarily involved. The court's decision thus seemed to revive the primary-situs rationale, despite its demise in *Professional & Business Men's Life* and in *Crystal Palace*.[108] It is submitted that the court reached a result contrary to the congressional policy of balancing the interests by deciding in favor of the union at the expense of the interests of neutral employers.

A subsequent decision reveals the impropriety of the court's holding. In *Local 36, Chemical Workers (Virginia-Carolina Chemical Corp.)*,[109] the Board allowed an employer to reserve a gate for the exclusive use of secondary employer's employees *after* the picketing had commenced. This result is directly opposite the result reached by the Court of Appeals for the Eighth Circuit in *Incorporated Oil*. The Board in *Virginia-Carolina* reasoned that since the geographical-location rationale of *Ryan* had been overruled, the question was whether or not the picketing was reasonable in light of the dual congressional intent embodied in section 8(b)(4)(A). The Board resolved this issue by relying upon the *Local 761, Electrical Workers (General Electric)*[110] decision, which

---

[106] Local 618, Automotive Employees v. NLRB, 249 F.2d 332, 337 (8th Cir. 1957).

[107] It can be inferred from the language used by the court that it did in fact rely upon the primary-situs rationale.

> The "an object" test [Moore Dry Dock test], applied here by the Board, is recognized as a proper test in cases where the picketing involved was not lawful primary picketing.

Id. at 334. The court later stated in distinguishing the Moore cases that:

> [t]he common situs cases [Moore cases] have some bearing upon the balancing of the primary right to strike against the prohibition of secondary boycotts, but do not bear as directly upon our present problem as the primary situs cases . . . .

Id. at 335-36.

[108] See discussion of Pure Oil, Ryan, and Crump in the court's opinion. *Id.* at 334-35.

[109] 126 N.L.R.B. 905 (1960), *enforced,* 47 L.R.R.M. 2493 (D.C. Cir.) (*per curiam*), *cert. denied,* 366 U.S. 949 (1961).

[110] 123 N.L.R.B. 1547 (1959), *enforced,* 278 F.2d 282 (D.C. Cir. 1960), *rev'd,* 366 U.S. 667 (1961).

had held that it was reasonable for a primary employer to limit the scope of the labor dispute by reserving a special gate for neutral employees. The Board then adopted the Trial Examiner's ruling that it was immaterial whether the separate gate was established before or after the picketing began.[111] Surely it is equally reasonable that an employer be allowed to withdraw one of the sites of a labor dispute from the primary situs by withdrawing all primary employees and primary activity from that location. If this reasoning had been applied to *Incorporated Oil,* the result in that case would not have implicitly revived the primary-situs rationale.

It can be seen that despite several cases that seemed to modify the *Moore* standards, only the *Washington* doctrine made any significant change in the application of those standards. The remaining cases reflect an attempt on the part of the Board to define and apply the existing standards to novel situations. Significantly, despite several maverick decisions, the Board consistently returned to the policy espoused in *Moore* of protecting the neutral employer as well as the union.

By 1959, the effective date of the Landrum-Griffin Act,[112] a consistent body of case law had emerged. It was a gradual process, punctuated with only a few major developments or shifts. Among these were the *Washington* doctrine and the application of the *Moore* standards to non-ambulatory common-situs picketing. As a result the statutory modifications were not designed to change the standards governing common-situs picketing.[113] Decisions

---

[111] 126 N.L.R.B. at 910.

[112] 73 Stat. 542 (1959), *as amended,* 29 U.S.C. 151-68 (1964).

[113] 29 U.S.C. § 158(b) (1964) of the amended Act, now governing common-situs picketing, reads as follows:

It shall be an unfair labor practice for a labor organization or its agents—
. . . .

(4) (i) to engage in, or to induce or encourage any individual employed by any person engaged in commerce or in an industry affecting commerce to engage in, a strike or a refusal in the course of his employment to use, manufacture, process, transport, or otherwise, handle or work on any goods, articles, materials, or commodities or to perform any services; or (ii) to threaten, coerce, or restrain any person engaged in commerce or in an industry affecting commerce, where in either case an object thereof is— . . . .

(B) forcing or requiring any person to cease using, selling, handling, transporting, or otherwise dealing in the products of any other producer, processor, or manufacturer, or to cease doing business with any other person, or forcing or requiring any other employer to

reached subsequent to the new amendments, but resulting from cases arising prior to their effective date, continued the process of developing a consistent analysis for situations that did not fit nicely under one of the pre-existing standards. The doctrines developed in these cases were consistent with the policy underlying *Moore,* and thus presumably with the intent of Congress in adopting the amendments to section 8(b)(4)(A).

The Separate-Gate Doctrine

The Board modified the law regulating common-situs picketing significantly in *United Steelworkers (Phelps Dodge Refining Co.)*.[114] This case arose prior to the effective date of Landrum-Griffin and, therefore, the Board's holding was based upon section 8(b)(4)(A). The union was engaged in a lawful strike against Phelps-Dodge. One week before the strike began, and in anticipation of it, Phelps-Dodge, the primary employer, constructed a separate gate to be used only by employees of independent construction contractors who were working at the Phelps-Dodge premises. When the strike began the union picketed the separate gate, causing the neutral employers to cease all work at the construction site. Phelps-Dodge then filed a complaint with the NLRB, alleging that the union had violated section 8(b)(4)(A).[115]

The Board held that the union's activity at the separate gate was an unfair labor practice.[116] The Court of Appeals for the Second Circuit, although enforcing the Board's order,[117] stated that picketing is not to be considered primary simply because it occurs at the premises of the primary employer.[118] The court reasoned that the separate gate was a device that afforded the neutral employer minimal protection and preserved the union's opportunity to publicize the dispute and to pressure the primary employer.[119] The

---

recognize or bargain with a labor organization as the representative of his employees unless such labor organization has been certified as the representative of such employees under the provisions of section 159 of this title: *Provided,* That nothing contained in this clause (B) shall be construed to make unlawful, where not otherwise unlawful, any primary strike or primary picketing; . . . .

[114] 126 N.L.R.B. 1367 (1960), *enforced,* 289 F.2d 591 (2d Cir. 1961).

[115] *Id.* at 1370.

[116] *Id.* at 1367.

[117] United Steelworkers v. NLRB, 289 F.2d 591 (2d Cir. 1961).

[118] *Id.* at 594.

[119] *Id.*

court's decision protected the neutral employer at the separate gate
by restricting the picketing to all other gates.

> There must be a separate gate marked and set apart from other
> gates; the work done by the men . . . must be unrelated to the
> normal operations of the employer and the work must be of a kind
> that would not, if done when the plant were engaged in its regular
> operations, necessitate curtailing these operations.[120]

This doctrine, like the one developed in *Washington,* is an exception to the *Moore* standards. The *Moore* standards, given the very
nature of the separate-gate situation, do not provide the neutral
employer with sufficient protection.[121] The Board, therefore, developed new standards to deal with this special problem. If the
gate is successfully reserved and is used exclusively by the intended
secondary employees, the *Moore* standards do not apply. Picketing
the reserved gate will always be viewed as secondary if the primary
employer meets the requirements of the above rule.

The *Local 761, Electrical Workers (General Electric)*[122] case
presented a complex problem that required clarification of the
separate-gate doctrine. Of the five gates at the primary employer's
plant, one was reserved for the exclusive use of employees of several independent contractors who performed renovating and maintenance work, which the regular employees were unable to perform. The various neutral employers did the construction work on
new buildings, installed and repaired heating and ventilating equipment, conducted retooling and rearranging operations, and did the
general maintenance work.[123] During a strike called by the union
representing General Electric's own employees, the union picketed
all five gates. The Board found that the union's object in picketing
the separate gate was to enmesh "employees of the neutral employer in its dispute with the Company."[124] The Board held that

---

[120] *Id.* at 595.

[121] It is conceivable that the union could exert undue pressure upon the
neutral employer while complying with all of the Moore standards. In the
separate-gate situation, the Moore standards would not prohibit the union
from picketing at all gates leading to the common situs.

[122] 123 N.L.R.B. 1547 (1959), *enforced,* 278 F.2d 282 (D.C. Cir. 1960), *rev'd,*
366 U.S. 667 (1961), *on remand,* 138 N.L.R.B. 342 (1962). (The Supreme
Court upheld the Board's separate-gate doctrine, but remanded the case to
the Board to determine whether the work done by those employers who used
the gate was related to that of the primary employer.

[123] *Id.* at 1548.

[124] *Id.* at 1550-51.

this was a violation of section 8(b)(4)(A). The Court of Appeals for the District of Columbia Circuit granted enforcement of the Board's order.[125] Review was then sought and granted in the Supreme Court.[126] The Supreme Court remanded the case to the NLRB with directions that the Board's original order be sustained unless the separate gate was used to a substantial extent by employees who performed work necessary to the normal operations of the manufacturer.[127] The Court recognized that the nature of the common-situs problem called for the development of new concepts to protect the interests of neutral employers as well as the picketing union at the primary situs. In remanding the case to the Board, the Court clarified the separate-gate doctrine in two significant ways. First, the Court stressed the central importance of the related-work concept by holding that picketing a separate gate is primary when the work of the secondary employer relates to that of the primary employer. The *Moore* standards do not apply if the three original *Phelps Dodge* requirements are met.[128] Secondly, the Court considered the implications arising from the mingled use of the gate by several independent contractors, some of whom performed related work, and indicated that if there were a mingled use of the reserved gate, the picketing would be primary and permissible unless the work was so insubstantial as to be *de minimus.*[129] On remand the Board applied this analysis and found that, since some of the contractors were doing related work, there was a mingled use of the gate.[130] The Board further found

---

[125] Local 761, Electrical Workers v. NLRB, 278 F.2d 282 (D.C. Cir. 1960), *rev'd,* 366 U.S. 667 (1961).

[126] 366 U.S. 667 (1961).

[127] *Id.* at 680-82.

[128] *Id.* at 681. The Court quoted from the decision of the Court of Appeals for the Second Circuit in the Phelps-Dodge case:

> There must be a separate gate marked and set apart from other gates; the work done by the men who use the gate must be unrelated to the normal operations of the employer and the work must be of a kind that would not, if done when the plant were engaged in its regular operations, necessitate curtailing those operations.

Id., citing United Steelworkers v. NLRB, 289 F.2d 591, 595 (2d Cir. 1961).

[129] *Id.* at 682.

[130] Local 761, Electrical Workers (General Electric), 138 N.L.R.B. 342 (1962). (The Board found that General Electric "employees had done non-conveyor work identical or substantially similar to that scheduled to be done by employees of the independent contractors in jobs whose contract prices totalled approximately $14,750.") *Id.* at 345-46.

that this work was not so insubstantial as to be *de minimus,* and thus, the union had not violated section 8(b)(4)(A).

The Related-Work Concept

The Board further modified the rules governing reserved-gate picketing in *Virginia-Carolina Chemical Corp.*[131] The issue in this case involved the first *Phelps Dodge* requirement—that there be a gate, marked and set apart from other gates for the exclusive use of neutral employers. This decision established that a gate could be properly reserved after picketing had commenced. If a gate is not properly reserved, then the *Moore* standards apply; thus, it is only when there has been a proper reservation of a gate that the related-work concept applies.[132] This result is consistent with the policy of protecting the neutral employer while preserving the union's right to exert pressure on the primary employer. The rationale conflicts, however, with that used by the Eighth Circuit in *Incorporated Oil.* [133] If a primary employer is able to limit the geographical scope of picketing by creating a reserved gate for employees of neutral employers, it is illogical not to allow him to limit the geographical scope of picketing by withdrawing his employees from one of several primary sites of the dispute. There is a minimal difference between the two situations. Clearly, in *Incorporated Oil* the secondary employer was not engaged in work related to the normal operations of the primary employer once all employees of the primary employer had been removed from the site. Had *Incorporated Oil* been decided on the same rationale as the *Virginia-Carolina* case, the union's right to publicize its dispute and to exert pressure on the primary employer would have been protected, without enmeshing the neutral employer in a dispute not of his own making.[134]

---

[131] 126 N.L.R.B. 905 (1960), *enforced,* 47 L.R.R.M. 2493 (D.C. Cir.) (*per curiam*) *cert. denied,* 366 U.S. 949 (1961).

[132] The employer in this case built a fence around the plant after the strike had commenced. He limited the use of one gate to the neutral employer. The union continued to picket the whole plant and all the gates. *Id.* at 908-09.

[133] See note 102 *supra* and accompanying text.

[134] The Supreme Court further refined the related work concept in Steelworkers v. NLRB, 376 U.S. 492 (1964). The Court held that the Union's right to picket at a separate gate is not prejudiced by violence in the picket line. The Court stated, inter alia, that the distinction between primary and secondary picketing rests upon the type of work being done by the neutral's employees and not upon the use of force in the picket line. The proper scope of inquiry is only into those matters that affect the balance between the conflicting interests of the unions and the neutral employer. *Id.* at 501.

Up to this point the decisions dealing with the related-work concept have involved the construction industry only as a secondary employer. *Building Trades Council (Markwell and Hartz)*[135] presented the Board with the opportunity to assess the applicability of the related-work concept to a primary employer in the construction industry. The union was engaged in a dispute with the general contractor at the construction site of a sewage disposal plant. After the picket line had been established, the general contractor reserved two of the three gates at the site for the exclusive use of the independent subcontractors. The union continued to picket all three gates. A complaint was filed with the NLRB, and the Board ruled that such activity constituted a violation of section 8(b) (4)(i) and (ii)(B) of the Act.[136]

The union argued unsuccessfully that the related-work concept applied and that their action was therefore primary and lawful. This argument raised the issue of whether or not the *Denver* case had been overruled by *General Electric*. *Denver* had held that the general contractor and the subcontractors are independent from one another for the purposes of section 8(b)(4)(A).[137] The related-work concept as applied in *General Electric* required that picketing at a separate gate used by neutral employers whose work was related to that of the primary employer was primary and therefore denied protection to those employers.[138] If the Board applied the related-work concept to *Markwell and Hartz,* it would, in effect, have overruled *Denver*. There would then be little justification for holding that in a separate-gate situation, the work of general contractor and subcontractor is related, whereas in other common-situs situations they are independent contractors and, thus, cannot be picketed in violation of 8(b)(4)(i) and (ii)(B). The result would be that picketing would always be primary if the neutral employer was a subcontractor and the primary employer was a general contractor.

The Board held that *Denver* prohibited the application of the related-work concept to the construction industry.[139] The Court of Appeals for the Sixth Circuit affirmed the Board's conclusions,[140]

---

[135] 155 N.L.R.B. 319 (1965), *enforced,* 387 F.2d 79 (5th Cir. 1967).

[136] *Id.* at 329-30.

[137] See note 58 *supra* and accompanying text.

[138] See note 122 *supra* and accompanying text.

[139] 155 N.L.R.B. at 327-28.

[140] Markwell & Hartz, Inc. v. NLRB, 387 F.2d 79 (5th Cir. 1967).

holding, *inter alia,* that *General Electric* did not deal with the construction industry and that the related-work concept was not a rule of general application. The court reasoned that the weight of the case law was too great to be overturned other than by the Congress or the Supreme Court.[141]

The Board's decision left separate-gate picketing in the construction industry to be governed by the *Moore* standards alone. Although *Phelps Dodge* and *General Electric* both involved secondary employees in the construction industry, the *Markwell and Hartz* rule applies only where both primary employer and the secondary employers, using the separate gate, are in the construction industry. Had it been held that the related-work concept applied to the construction industry, the Board would have been forced to reach one of two conclusions: either it would have had to ignore the realities of the situation and hold that such work is unrelated and, thus, that separate-gate picketing is secondary; or it would have had to hold all such work related and, thus, that all picketing at a separate gate is primary. In either case, the result would have been unsatisfactory. The rule would apply automatically on an across-the-board basis in the construction industry. The Board has chosen instead to govern separate-gate picketing in the construction industry through the *Moore* standards.[142] Such a policy provides far more flexibility than would a rigid application of the related-work concept. The resultant standards allow the unions to picket a separate gate provided that they comply with certain safeguards, which minimize the effect of the picketing on neutral employers.

The final holding in *Markwell and Hartz* was that this specific picketing violated the *Moore* standard—that such activity be conducted reasonably close to the situs of the dispute.[143] The standard applied was flexible, and neither prohibited nor allowed *all* separate-gate picketing in the construction industry. The application of the *Moore* standards provides for the protection of the interests of all concerned parties. The finding that the picketing was not reasonably close to the situs was based on the particular facts in the case and was not meant to be aplied on a *per se* basis throughout the construction industry.[144]

---

[141] *Id.* at 83.

[142] 155 N.L.R.B. at 323-27.

[143] *Id.* at 326-27.

[144] *Id.* at 327.

The case law reveals, however, that the construction industry is most frequently involved in reserved-gate problems as a secondary employer. The rules governing separate-gate picketing in this situation were further defined in the recent *Janesville Typographical Local 197 (Gazette Printing)*[145] case. The union's dispute with Gazette, the primary employer, involved certain work-preservation problems caused by the construction of a new plant housing several labor-saving devices. The new facility was to be constructed on the same premises as the old facility, which remained in operation while the construction work proceeded. The union picketed the plant and a gate reserved for the construction workers.[146] The issue presented was whether the work being done by the secondary employer (i.e., construction of the new plant) was related to that of the primary employer. The Board held that the construction work was not related to the normal operations of the primary employer, even though the construction work may have been related to the issue of the dispute between the union and the primary employer.[147] The fact that the union's dispute involved the work being done by the secondary employer was not sufficient to overcome the separate-gate doctrine.[148] The Board reasoned that all work done by neutral employers on the primary employer's premises could eventually be tied to an increased efficiency in the primary employer's operations and, thus, to the dispute between the union and the primary employer. The Board concluded that to allow the union to defend its picketing upon such a use of the related-work concept would be to destroy its utility. The Board, therefore, held that the union had violated section 8(b)(4)(i) and (ii)(B), and thereby retained the viability of the related-work concept.[149]

It can be seen from the three modifications developed above—the *Washington* doctrine, the separate-gate doctrine, and the related-work concept—that the Board did not regress from the policy underlying the *Moore* standards. Rather, it is clear that the Board developed in these three situations additional protection for the neutral employer. The *Washington* doctrine, in effect, limited the right of the union to picket at an ambulatory situs, and there-

---

[145] 173 N.L.R.B. 917, 69 L.R.R.M. 1457 (1968).

[146] *Id.*

[147] *Id.* at 1458.

[148] *Id.* at 1458-59.

[149] *Id.* at 1460.

fore limited the application of the *Moore* standards to those situations where the primary employer could not be picketed "effectively" at his place of business. The separate-gate doctrine further limited the power of the union by allowing the primary employer to withdraw a section of his premises from the primary-situs of the dispute. In this manner, the neutral employers working on the premises of the primary employer can continue their business without being subjected to any pressure by the union. The related-work concept clarified the scope of the separate-gate doctrine by defining the type of work that a neutral employer would have to be doing before the separate-gate doctrine would not apply. Although this concept does not afford additional protection to the neutral employer, it does clarify the rights of the neutrals with respect to the separate-gate doctrine. The three modifications of the *Moore* standards do not, however, alter the underlying congressional policy embodied in section 8(b)(4); rather, they manifest the continued policy of balancing the interests of the neutral employer and the union.

NEW-FRONTIER ALTERATION OF THE STANDARDS

The appointment of new personnel to the NLRB by the late President John F. Kennedy stimulated changes in the application and interpretation of the case law relating to common-situs picketing.[150] The modifications that have been made are still in effect today. By the beginning of the Kennedy administration, the *Moore* standards had become the cornerstone of the principles regulating common-situs picketing. The developments since that time have not eliminated the *Moore* standards, but rather have introduced subtle modifications, which affect the strength of the proscription on secondary boycotts as set forth in Section 8(b)(4)(i) and (ii)(B) of the Act.

Washington Doctrine Overruled

The most significant change occurred in *Electrical Workers Local 861 (Plauche Electric, Inc.)*,[151] an ambulatory picketing case. The

---

[150] Chairman Frank McCulloch took office on March 7, 1961, N.Y. Times, Feb. 5, 1961, at 38, col. 1; Member Gerald Brown took office on April 14, 1961, id., Mar. 15, 1961, at 45 col. 2; Member John Fanning, an Eisenhower appointee, rounded out the New-Frontier majority.

[151] 135 N.L.R.B. 250 (1962).

primary employer, Plauche Electric, was involved in a dispute with the union concerning Plauche's agreement to hire non-union employees for a job to be performed on the premises of a neutral employer. The union picketed the jobsite where Plauche's employees were working, but did not picket the primary employer's place of business, which was located near the jobsite and to which Plauche employees usually reported twice a day. The picketing prevented the suppliers and employees of neutral employers from entering the jobsite. The majority of the Board held that there was no violation of the Act.[152] In reaching this decision, the Board misconstrued *Washington Coca-Cola* to the extent that it chose not to apply the "effectiveness" test as a pre-condition to the *Moore* standards. The Board rationalized this approach on the basis that a per se application of the *Washington* doctrine would be too rigid.[153] The Board attempted to add weight to its rationale by reasoning that *Pittsburgh Plate Glass* was inconsistent with *Washington*.[154] Examination of those two cases, however, reveals that they are quite consistent. The Board in *Pittsburgh Plate* held that if the union could not effectively picket the primary employer's place of business, the picketing at an ambulatory situs or at the premises of a secondary employer was permissible.[155] This decision, based upon a consideration of the effectiveness of picketing at the primary employer's place of business, was, therefore, quite consistent with the correct interpretation of *Washington*.

The Board's decision in *Plauche* also affected the application of the *Moore* standards.

> In overruling *Washington Coca-Cola* we do not, of course, hold that the place of picketing is irrelevant in determining the legality of the picketing. We shall in the future, as we have with court

---

[152] *Id.* at 256.

[153] The Board assumed that the Washington doctrine required a per se ruling that picketing at the premises of a neutral was a violation of the Act if the primary employer had premises near the dispute. It is difficult to see how the Board arrived at the "rigid rule" that they so adeptly knocked down. As discussed in text accompanying note 81 *supra*, the "effectiveness" standard in Washington allows the Board to determine on each occasion whether or not the union can effectively picket the primary employer at the primary's place of business. Under the facts found by the Board, it is doubtful whether the union could have picketed effectively at the primary's place of business (i.e., the primary's employees reported only twice a day and on some days did not even report at the primary's place of business). *Id.* at 251-52.

[154] *Id.* at 254. *See* Painters Local 193 (Pittsburgh Plate Glass), 110 N.L.R.B. 455 (1954) and discussion in text accompanying note 83 *supra*.

[155] See note 84 *supra*.

> approval in the past, consider the place of picketing as one circum-
> stance, among others, in determining an object of the picketing. . . .
>   . . . .
>
>   . . . Accordingly, the picketing to be lawful had to accord with
> the *Moore Dry Dock* standards. These standards also are not to be
> applied on an indiscriminate "per se" basis, but are to be regarded
> merely as aids in determining the underlying question of statutory
> violation.[156]

This analysis can be fairly criticized both on the ground that the
Board viewed the *Washington* rules as being more rigid than they
actually were,[157] and on the ground that the Board unnecessarily
created confusion as to the application of the *Moore* standards.

Dissenting Board Members Rodgers and Leedom argued that the
Plauche case could have been decided under the *Washington* doctrine with results that would have been equitable to all parties.[158]
They viewed the majority opinion as completely overruling *Washington,* despite the claims by the majority that it was only being
partially overruled.[159] The dissent explained that the "effectiveness" standard encompassed adequate flexibility, and therefore
Washington should have been retained.

> Our colleagues do not say the Respondent could not have effectively
> picketed at Plauche's place of business. If they disagree with our
> conclusion on that question, that would be a reason for disagree-
> ing with our ultimate conclusion that this record supports a finding
> of a violation under the principles set forth above [*Washintgon*
> doctrine]; it is not, however, a reason for abandoning those
> principles.[160]

In effect, the majority applied two existent rules in ways that
radically alter the law governing common-situs picketing. The
Washington doctrine provided a flexible standard that gave both
unions and employers a clear idea of what limitations were placed

---

[156] 135 N.L.R.B. at 254-55 (footnotes omitted).

[157] See discussion in text accompanying notes 86-101 *supra.*

[158] 135 N.L.R.B. at 258.

[159] The dissenting Board members argued that under the Washington
"effectiveness standard" the union should be limited to the primary employer's place of business. From this basis they then argue that the majority is not only overruling a per se application of the Washington doctrine
but is also effectively overruling any consideration of whether or not the
union could picket the primary employer effectively at his principal place of
business. *Id.* at 258-59.

[160] *Id.* at 259 n.14.

upon their prerogatives. When the Board overruled *Washington,* not only did it reject a doctrine by which the conflicting interests of parties present at a common situs had been successfully balanced, but also it failed to provide new standards by which the rights of parties in such situations could be determined.[161] Such standards are desirable because they serve to maximize consistency in the determination of the rights of parties in litigation. They also serve the more important function of preventing litigation: first, by giving notice to unions of the limits of permissible action in their dispute with the primary employer, and secondly, by determining the legal scope of a neutral employer's protection at a common situs.

In addition, the Board unnecessarily created uncertainty by holding that the *Moore* standards are to be regarded as aids in determining the legality of picketing at a common situs and are not to be applied on a per se basis.[162] The *Moore* standards have never been applied on an indiscriminate ad hoc basis. It seems plain that the Board's emphasis on the *Moore* standards was intended to create a change in the way those standards were to be applied to common-situs picketing. The ultimate consequences of this intended change, however, were left unclear.

Truck Drivers Local 728 (Brown Transport Corp.)[163] presented the Board with a situation remarkably similar to that in *Southwestern Motor Transport.*[164] The union, engaged in a dispute with Brown, picketed the company's business headquarters. Picketing was also conducted at the premises of neutral employers while the primary employer's trucks were present making pick-ups and deliveries. The pickets were instructed to picket at the gate nearest the trucks if they were denied permission to enter the premises of neutral employers. Often such picketing was out of the sight of the employees of the primary employer.[165] The Board found that the

---

[161] The Board, by partially overruling Washington in a situation where the case could have been decided under the effectiveness rationale, by-passed an opportunity to further define that standard. By reducing the Washington doctrine to "a factor" to be considered with the Moore standards, the Board left the law with regard to picketing in the Plauche and Washington situations in a state of flux. As a result of the Plauche decision, it is difficult to to make even an educated guess as to the legality of picketing at a neutral's premises in the Washington situation.

[162] 135 N.L.R.B. at 255.

[163] 144 N.L.R.B. 590 (1963), *rev'd,* 344 F.2d 30 (5th Cir. 1964).

[164] 115 N.L.R.B. 981 (1956). See note 95 *supra* and accompanying text.

[165] 144 N.L.R.B. at 600-01.

delivery drivers spent at least as much time at the primary employer's permanent place of business as did the drivers in the
Southwestern case.[166]

Despite prior case law [167] and the ruling in *Plauche* that the
existence of a primary place of business that could be effectively
picketed is to be considered as one of the *Moore* standards,[168] the
Board found that the union's activity was primary and therefore
beyond the reach of the statutory prohibition.[169] A majority of
the Board ignored the new *Moore* standard created in *Plauche*,
and also neglected the fact that the picketing at the premises of
neutral employers was often conducted in areas where it could not
be seen by primary employees. Member Leedom, who dissented in
Plauche, again disagreed with the majority. He argued that the
picketing was illegal both under the *Washington* doctrine and under
the *Plauche* rules.[170]

The Court of Appeals for the Fifth Circuit, in accord with the
dissenting member, held that the Board had ignored the *Moore*
standard requiring that picketing be limited to a place reasonably
close to the situs of the dispute.[171]

> . . . This must necessarily mean that the picketing must be
> within the sight of the picketed employee of the primary employer.
> Otherwise there would be absolutely no basis for holding that the
> picketing was for the purpose of persuading him rather than the
> other persons who were within view of his sign.[172]

The court criticized the Board for the result it reached, observing

---

[166] The Board in *Southwestern* held that since the truck drivers were at the
primary employer's plant at least twice a day, the Washington doctrine
applied and the union was violating section 8(b)(4)(A). In Brown, the
dissent argued that the facts showed that the trucks were on the premises
several times a day and that they could be effectively picketed there. 144
N.L.R.B. at 593-94.

[167] *See* Washington Coca-Cola, 107 N.L.R.B. 299 (1953); Pittsburgh Plate
Glass Co., 110 N.L.R.B. 455 (1954); Southwestern Motor Transport, 115
N.L.R.B. 981 (1956). See also note 93 *supra*.

[168] *See* 135 N.L.R.B. at 253.

[169] 144 N.L.R.B. at 592-93.

[170] *Id.* at 594. The dissenting Board member argued that the union had
violated the Washington doctrine, because they could have picketed effectively
at the primary employer's plant, and that they had violated the policy underlying section 8(b)(4)(i) and (ii)(B) by not limiting the picketing at the
neutral employer's premises to the primary employees. *Id.*

[171] Brown Transport Corp. v. NLRB, 334 F.2d 30 (5th Cir. 1964).

[172] *Id.* at 38.

that *Plauche* modified, but did not overrule, *Washington*. The court reasoned:

> . . . It must be borne in mind that the modification of the Washington Coca-Cola Bottling Company holding by the subsequent Plauche case does not eliminate the factor of presence of a primary place of business where picketing can be readily carried on as one of the important factors to be considered by the Board or by the Courts when faced with a decision as to whether, under all the circumstances, it can be held that the improper pressure on third party employers is not an object of the ambulatory picketing.[173]

In so ruling, the court emphasized that the Board had failed to follow its own decision in *Plauche* by ignoring the existence of a primary premises that could be picketed effectively.

In its decision, the Board made one statement that should clarify the doubt created in *Plauche* as to the status of the *Moore* rules.

> We recognize that the *Moore Dry Dock* standards "are not to be applied on an indiscriminate *'per se'* basis" . . . , and that mere outward compliance with such standards may not be used as a shield where independent proof exists that the picketing was actually aimed at achieving unlawful secondary objectives over and beyond such incidental effects as might normally be a concomitant of legitimate primary picketing.[174]

The significance of this language is that the *Moore* standards are not the only determinatives of the legality of common-situs picketing. If the *Moore* standards are violated, the union will have violated the Act; if the standards are met, however, independent evidence of an illegal, secondary objective will be received to determine the legality of such activity.

The court's application of *Washington*, despite the Board's contrary holding in *Plauche*, revealed that the prior case law had remained intact. The problems in *Plauche*, *Brown* and subsequent cases did not arise because the principles set forth in the case law were either weak or improper, but simply because the Board was not properly applying and enforcing the case law. In the following cases, the standards are again clearly set forth and a decision is reached that is seemingly based upon those standards, but often the decision reached conflicts with the policies underlying those standards.

---

[173] *Id.* at 37-38.

[174] 144 N.L.R.B. at 592, citing Electrical Workers Local 861 (Plauche Electric, Inc.), 135 N.L.R.B. 250, 251 (1962).

Modification of the Moore Standards—Substantial Compliance

The *Local 3, Electrical Workers (New Power Wire and Electric Corp.)*[175] decision followed both *Plauche* and *Brown Transport*. As a result of its dispute for recognition with New Power, the union picketed the company headquarters and other sites where employees of the primary employer were engaged in wiring operations in residential apartment houses. During the early stages of the strike, the pickets went inside the apartment buildings, but the picketing was subsequently confined to the front of the buildings involved. Picketing continued during prolonged periods when no employees were working at these sites, although supervisors visited the sites daily. It was established that the absence of employees from these buildings was due to the effectiveness of the strike. When the work at a site was completed, the pickets were withdrawn.[176] Reversing the trial examiner, the Board found no violation of the *Moore* standards.[177] Consideration was not given to the new *Moore* test created in *Plauche*. Instead, the Board relied upon the language in *Plauche* that the *Moore* rules were to be regarded only as aids in determining the legality of picketing and held that the activity here "complied substantially" with the *Moore Dry Dock* conditions for permissible, primary picketing at a common situs.[178]

The Board in *New Power* invented a requirement of substantial compliance—a requirement that is not supported by any prior case law nor by the overriding policy of balancing the interests of unions with those of neutral employees. Such a drastic departure from the established body of law cannot be justified by the fact that the law has evolved on a case-by-case basis and new problems, such as separate-gate picketing, have generated new solutions. The facts presented were not unique. The requirements of the standards were clear. The Board failed to apply its own rules correctly

---

[175] 144 N.L.R.B. 1089 (1963).

[176] *Id.* at 1091.

[177] *Id.* at 1092.

[178] *Id.* at 1092-93. The trial examiner had found that the picketing in the absence of the primary employer's employees from the neutral's premises "for substantial periods of time demonstrates that Respondent's picketing was directed toward the unlawful inducement of employees of secondary employers . . . ." *Id.* at 1093. The Board held that this was only one of the factors to be considered and that it "does not require a finding that the Company is not engaged in its normal business at the common situs or that the common situs is not the situs of the primary dispute." *Id.* at 1093.

and the result contradicts the policy underlying those rules. Moreover, a rule of "substantial compliance" creates uncertainty in an area where clear guidelines are desired. An indefinite requirement such as "substantial compliance" disrupts those guidelines already established and undermines the policy enunciated in *Denver* of balancing the conflicting interests of unions and neutral employers.[179]

It is submitted that the decision in *New Power* was more questionable than the decision in *Incorporated Oil*.[180] The Board in *New Power* stated that

> [i]n a situation such as this, the absence of the primary employer's employees is merely one of the factors to be evaluated in determining whether the situs of the primary dispute is located at the common situs during the picketing, and whether the primary employer is then engaged in his normal business at the site.[181]

At least in *Incorporated Oil* the union picketed premises owned by the primary employer while there were no employees of the primary employer present. In *New Power* the union picketed the premises of neutral employers while there were no employees of the primary employer present. Although title to property should not be determinative of common-situs issues, the fact that the picketing occurred at premises owned by neutral employers reveals the uncertainty and imbalance the Board has generated by decreasing the protection that the Act affords neutrals. The Board, in rationalizing its result, relied upon *General Electric's*[182] determination that common-situs picketing problems call for an evolutionary process to generate a rational response, rather than a quick, definitive answer.[183] The Board appears to have engaged in the very process that it condemned and has created a quick, definitive answer that contradicts the body of precedent that had been developed.

In a subsequent case, *Electrical Workers Local 861 (Brownfield Electric, Inc.)*,[184] the Board undertook to redefine its holding in

[179] See note 58 *supra* and accompanying text.

[180] Local 618, Automotive Employees (Incorporated Oil Co.), 116 N.L.R.B. 1844 (1956), *enforcement denied*, 249 F.2d 332 (8th Cir. 1957). The Board held in this case that the union could picket a primary's retail gas station despite the fact that the only employees present were neutrals to the dispute.

[181] 144 N.L.R.B. at 1093.

[182] See note 122 *supra* and accompanying text.

[183] 144 N.L.R.B. at 1093.

[184] 145 N.L.R.B. 1163 (1964).

New Power. The facts of this case were essentially the same as *New Power*, with the single exception that in this case the primary employer had no permanent place of business near the area of the jobsite. The primary employer was Brownfield, who was a subcontractor of Smith Construction working at an apartment building jobsite. The union established a picket line at the jobsite. The picketing continued for three days, despite the fact that the union knew that no employees of the primary employer were present. Despite the contentions of the General Counsel that such activity constituted a violation of the *Moore* requirement that the primary employer be engaged in its normal business operations at the situs of the dispute, the Board held on the basis of *New Power* that there was no violation of the Act.[185]

> Picketing which is lawful primary picketing is not turned into unlawful secondary picketing because the picketing is effective against the primary employer and its employees [citing *New Power*], or because the primary employer is seeking to prevent the picketing by turning out its employees. Under such circumstances, absent proof of an unlawful object beyond those normal incidental effects of a primary picket line, a union may be engaged in lawful primary picketing despite the absence of primary employees.[186]

The Board relied upon the fact that the primary employer was scheduled to work at the jobsite for three of the four days that the picketing was conducted. The Board also relied upon testimony by the general contractor's superintendent to the effect that a reason why no employees of the primary were present at a later date was because he desired to prevent the pickets from returning.[187] It would appear that the Board drew the inference that the superintendent prevented the primary employer's employees from being at the jobsite as a response to the union picket line. As pointed out in the dissenting opinion of Member Leedom, the majority opinion

> comes dangerously close to holding that the mere existence of a subcontract gives a union the unalloyed right to picket a construction project in support of its primary dispute with the subcontractor at any and all times until the subcontract has been fulfilled.[188]

---

[185] *Id.* at 1166.

[186] *Id.* (footnotes omitted).

[187] *Id.*

[188] *Id.* at 1167.

Such a holding would directly contradict a long line of cases, beginning with *Denver* [189] and including *Markwell and Hartz,* that specifically hold that in the construction industry a contractor and a subcontractor are each independent contractors and that each should be afforded the full protection of the Act. Such a decision would, in effect, strip the *Moore* standards of much of their vitality and deny interested parties any certainty in dealing with secondary boycotts and common-situs picketing.

Independent Proof of Secondary Objective

Electrical Workers Local 480 v. NLRB (Gulf Coast Building and Supply Co.) [190] reaffirmed the ruling in *Brown Transport* that compliance with the *Moore* rules will not prevent the Board from finding a violation of the Act where independent evidence indicates the existence of prohibited, secondary objectives.

The Board and the Court of Appeals for the District of Columbia Circuit relied upon independent proof to find a violation of the Act, despite compliance with the *Moore* standards. Although there has not been any case that has allowed independent proof of the legality of picketing after a finding that one of the *Moore* standards had been violated, in light of *New Power* and *Brownfield,* it would not be unreasonable to expect that the Board and the courts would be willing to so rule. It is, however, somewhat difficult to imagine any circumstance that would permit independent proof of legality where the picketing has violated *Moore.* In fact, such an analysis undercuts the "substantial compliance" analysis used in *New Power* and in *Brownfield* as well as the "one of the factors" analysis of *Plauche.* The requirements of the *Moore* standards were not met in those cases, and there was no independent proof of legality, yet the Board upheld the picketing as being primary and as being in substantial compliance with *Moore.*

Failure to meet any of the *Moore* standards is indicative of an illegal, secondary objective. The *Moore* standards protect the interests of both the union and the neutral employer by allowing the union to picket at a common situs with certain restrictions that minimize the effect of such activity on the employees of the secondary employer. At the same time, by allowing this slightly restricted picketing at a common situs, the standards impinge upon the

---

[189] See note 58 *supra* and accompanying text.

[190] 172 N.L.R.B. No. 64, 69 L.R.R.M. 1054 (1968), *enforced,* 413 F.2d 1085 (1969).

neutral employer's rights to remain free from disputes in which he is not involved. The rules are intended to accomplish a balance between the interests of unions and neutral, secondary employees. The breakdown has not occurred in the rules themselves, but in the application of the rules.

Clear Misapplication of Moore

The *United Steelworkers Local 6991 (Auburndale Freezer Corp.)*[191] case presented the Board with a complicated fact pattern that resulted in a misapplication of the standards. The Auburndale Freezer Corporation operated a cold-storage warehouse in which citrus processors stored citrus concentrate. The union was engaged in a dispute with one of these processors, Cypress. Picketing occurred at the premises of Cypress and also at the Auburndale warehouse. Cypress employees had never worked at the warehouse, and during the course of the strike and the picketing, no Cypress trucks came to Auburndale, and no Cypress goods were shipped from Auburndale.

The Board found no violation of *Moore* and upheld the union's picketing activity.[192] In reaching this conclusion the Board specificially ruled that the decision was not based on the "Ally doctrine"[193] and that Auburndale was not an ally of Cypress. The Board recognized the situation presented as a common-situs-picketing problem, which required application of the *Moore* standards.[194] The Board relied on *New Power* and held that the absence of the employees of the struck employer is only one factor to be considered.

Even if one were to accept *New Power* as controlling, its application to the facts in this case was obviously improper. Unlike *New Power*, the employees of the primary employer had never worked at the premises of the secondary employer. The Board's holding that the Auburndale premises constituted a common situs of the dispute was based upon the finding that the Auburndale warehouse was part of the Cypress operation.[195] The Board based

---

[191] 177 N.L.R.B. No. 108, 71 L.R.R.M. 1503 (1969).

[192] *Id.* at 1505.

[193] The Ally doctrine is an exception to section 8(b)(4)(i) and (ii)(B), whereby a secondary employer loses his neutrality for performing struck work or for being a joint owner of the primary employer's business, and therefore, becomes susceptible to union pressure. See Lesnick, *supra* note 3.

[194] 71 L.R.R.M. at 1504-05.

[195] *Id.*

its findings on facts that indicated that the warehouse had become an integral part of the struck employer's production process. In effect, the Board ruled that because of this integral relationship between Cypress and Auburndale, there had been a substantial compliance with the *Moore* requirements, even though this relationship was not sufficiently strong to make Auburndale an "ally" of Cypress. In effect, the Board subjected Auburndale to the same penalties and the consequent lack of protection as if it had been found to be an "ally." [196]

There is little justification for this result. The facts in *Auburndale* show a clear violation of the *Moore* standards. The Auburndale premises were not the situs of the dispute.[197] As the dissenting opinion of Chairman McCulloch and Member Brown pointed out, the majority overstepped the bounds of the present case law.

> Our understanding of the [New Power Wire] decision cited [by the majority] and similar precedents is that they have reference to situations in which employees of the primary employer are normally engaged in tasks at the picketed premises but are absent because of a strike, . . . or for some other similar reason. Here no employees of Cypress, the primary employer with whom Respondents had their dispute, had ever performed tasks at the picketed premises. Such employees were not simply "absent." They never were there. In this situation, the only possible thrust of Respondents' picketing appeal must have been directed to the neutral Auburndale, to the neutral employees engaged in warehousing tasks, or to the neutral employees of Auburndale's other customers. This is the classic example of the secondary boycott proscribed by the statute.[198]

In effect they argued that the Board's decision is based solely on the "mere presence of a primary employer's goods on the premises of a neutral employer" [199] and that this result constitutes a major abuse under the case law and under the Act. The Fifth Circuit Court agreed with the Board dissenters.[200] In a divided decision, the court held that the picketing was prohibited by the plain terms of the statute.

---

[196] Compare the holding here with that in Douds v. Metropolitan Fed'n of Architects, 75 F. Supp. 672 (S.D.N.Y. 1948).

[197] The Trial Examiner found that during the entire time of the strike there were no employees of the primary employer at the neutral employer's premises. 71 L.R.R.M. at 1504.

[198] *Id.* at 1506 (dissenting opinion).

[199] *Id.*

[200] Auburndale Freezer Corp. v. NLRB, 75 L.R.R.M. 2752 (5th Cir. 1970).

CONCLUDING REMARKS

The effect of the NLRB majority decision in *Auburndale* is to open entirely new areas that had previously been protected to secondary pressure through picketing. The normal business relationship between two independent employers becomes a sufficient basis for the existence of a common situs and for the finding of compliance with the *Moore* standards. If the Board continues to follow the principle established here, neutral employers will find little protection under the Act, and the union's right to publicize its dispute and to exert pressure on the primary employer will have been expanded to an extent not only undesirable, but dangerous as well. The earliest cases dealing with common-situs picketing distinguished between picketing that occurred at the premises of the primary employer and picketing that occurred at the premises of the secondary employer. These standards were inflexible. The roving-situs doctrine was developed to allow picketing at the premises of secondary employers when it was found that the situs of the dispute was ambulatory. The scope of permissible ambulatory picketing was expanded by the *Moore* standards, which also established certain safeguards for the neutral, secondary employer. Following the gradual demise of the primary-situs rationale and the enunciation of a policy of attaining the dual congressional objectives of balancing the conflicting interests of unions and neutrals, the *Moore* standards were established as the sole criteria for determining the legality of common-situs picketing. The *Washington* doctrine set forth further safeguards for neutrals and unions in ambulatory common-situs-picketing situations. Also, the Board and courts had created a new body of rules governing picketing at a separate gate at the primary employer's premises.

By the time Landrum-Griffin was enacted in 1959, the body of law governing common-situs picketing was well established. The rules were not rigid. The *Moore* standards were sufficiently flexible to accommodate the unique case, although preserving predictability and consistency. The standards were not intended to be used as a shield, and compliance with *Moore* could not prevent a finding of illegal, secondary activity in the face of independent proof to that effect. The Board in *Washington* developed an additional standard, the "effectiveness" test, which served to protect union interests in publicizing the dispute and in exerting pressure on the primary employer where the union could not effectively do so at the premises of the primary employer.

Despite the fact that the *Moore* standards have remained intact and that according to the Board, the *Washington* doctrine has only been modified, the common-situs picketing principles are very much different today from what they were in 1959. The new amendments were meant to have no effect in this area; the prior case law has not been overruled; and yet a radically different result is reached under these same laws today. Although the *Moore* standards are referred to in almost every recent decision, action that clearly violates the *Moore* standards is upheld, as the Board and the courts side-step the issues.

Common-situs picketing is an extremely complex area of labor law. The Board and the courts are entrusted with safeguarding interests that clash at any common situs. The case law has emerged gradually, and these decisions have firmly established the necessity for a flexible approach to such problems. There is no doubt that flexibility is an essential element in the fair administration of the law in any area and especially in an area as multifaceted and volatile as common-situs picketing. But flexibility must be tempered with consistency and predicability. The policy underlying the *Moore* standards and the Act is to create a balance between unions and neutrals in a common-situs situation. Part of the function of the Board and courts in this area is to supply guidelines that will enable parties to conform their actions to the requirements of the law so as to avoid litigation. Excessive degrees, either of rigidity or flexibility, are equally undesirable. A case-by-case study of the NLRB's "case by case" approach reveals that the decisions create an excessive degree of flexibility and thereby sacrifice the much-needed element of clarity. Even though the recent decisions tend to support the particular picketing activity involved, the long-term interests of neither neutral employers nor unions are actually enhanced. It serves the interests of both parties to avoid costly and time-consuming litigation. The imposition of definite boundaries on these interests serves to benefit both parties as long as the boundaries are equitably defined.

CHAPTER III

The Ally Doctrine

A secondary boycott directly involves three parties: the union, the primary employer, with whom the union has a dispute; and a secondary employer, upon whom the union exerts pressure in order to hasten a favorable settlement of its dispute with the primary employer. In such situations, the crucial question in determining the legality or illegality of the union's activity in relation to the secondary employer is whether that employer is a neutral party. It is only when that secondary party is neutral to the primary dispute that a secondary boycott arises.

This requirement of neutrality is not specifically provided for under the Act. The proviso of the 1959 Amendments merely serves to safeguard the union's right to engage in a primary strike or picketing. Under the original union unfair labor practice section of the Taft-Hartley Amendments of 1947 secondary activity was proscribed.

It was from the 1947 provisions that the Board and courts developed the requirement of neutrality and the sanctity of primary union activity which are fundamental to the "ally doctrine." In explaining the above language, the late Senator Taft laid the foundation upon which the ally doctrine was built.

> This provision makes it unlawful to resort to a secondary boycott to injure the business of a third person who is wholly unconcerned in the disagreement between an employer and his employees.[1]

Initially, the ally doctrine was a rather ambiguous concept that allowed unions to engage in secondary type activity where the third party employer is not neutral. The ally doctrine stated that where a secondary employer is closely related to the primary employer and the dispute with the union, he loses his neutrality and may be treated as a primary party to the dispute. Over the years, however, the concept has been refined by NLRB and court decisions. Three basic situations have evolved in which the ally doctrine has been applied. The secondary's performance of "farmed-out struck work" has become one basis for granting the union leave to conduct a strike or picketing against a secondary employer. The

---

[1] 93 Cong. Rec. 4198 (1947).

remaining two situations arise where the business relationship of the primary employer and the secondary are so intertwined as to create either a "straight line operation" or a "co-employer situation." These refinements, however, have not always served the interests of maintaining an equitable balance between union and secondary employer rights.

The fundamental principles underlying the Board and court policy regarding secondary boycotts have been to maintain a balance between the rights of unions to engage in primary activity and to publicize their labor disputes and the rights of secondary employers to remain free from direct involvement in the disputes of others. This policy underlies the ally doctrine. Where the secondary employer is allied with the primary employer the union has a complete defense to charges of a secondary boycott. Much ambiguity and uncertainty still surrounds the interpretation and especially the application of the ally doctrine. The confused state of current law hampers stable industrial relations and encourages the expansion of a labor dispute beyond the parties of immediate concern. This chapter examines the history and development of the ally doctrine in the light of the policies set forth in the law and the conflicting rights involved.

GENESIS OF THE ALLY DOCTRINE

The origin of the ally doctrine lies in the case of *Douds v. Metropolitan Federation of Architects Local 231.*[2] It involved farmed-out struck work and, to a certain extent, elements of common control. Ebasco Services, Inc. and Project Engineering Co. both dealt in engineering services. Before the union's strike against Ebasco, Project had secured subcontracts from Ebasco to perform certain tasks. After the strike began, Project took on an appreciably greater amount of work from Ebasco. Some of this was sent to Project for completion after Ebasco had begun it. The Project employees performing the subcontract work were supervised by Ebasco personnel. After Project refused the union request to stop this work, picketing took place at Project's premises. The issue facing the court was whether the union's activity constituted a secondary boycott. The court concluded that the nature of the relationship between Ebasco and Project precluded a finding of neutrality and that the union's activity did not therefore violate the Act.

---

[2] 75 F. Supp. 672 (S.D.N.Y. 1948).

> To suggest that Project had no interest in the dispute between Ebasco and its employees is to look at the form and remain blind to substance. In every meaningful sense it made itself party to the contest. Manifestly, it was not an innocent bystander, nor a neutral. It was firmly allied to Ebasco and it was its conduct as ally of Ebasco which directly provoked the union's action.[3]

The court did not predicate this decision on grounds of common control and supervision of Project people by Ebasco. It certainly would seem reasonable, however, to assume that this was one of the several elements considered by the court when it decided that Project had "made itself party to the contest" in every significant way. Thus, this case supplied some support for the subsequent line of cases that would follow the straight line or the co-employer theories of alliance.

The specific grounds for the court's decision that the two employers had become allies was the performance of farmed-out struck work:

> The evidence is abundant that Project's employees did work, which, but for the strike of Ebasco's employees would have been done by Ebasco. The economic effect upon Ebasco's employees was precisely that which would flow from Ebasco's hiring strike-breakers to work on its own premises. The conduct of the union in inducing Project's employees to strike is not different in kind from its conduct in inducing Ebasco employees to strike. If the latter is not amenable to judicial restraint, neither is the former. In encouraging a strike at Project the union was not extending its activity to a front remote from the immediate dispute, but to one intimately and indeed inextricably united to it.[4]

The *Metropolitan Architects* decision established an important exception to the statutory ban on secondary boycots. The court's reasoning received the recognition and approval of Senator Taft.

> The secondary boycott ban . . . is not intended to apply to a case where (the secondary employer) is, in effect, in cahoots with or acting as a part of the primary employer . . . , where the secondary employer is so closely allied to the primary employer as to amount to an alter ego situation or an employer relationship. The spirit of the Act is not intended to protect a man who . . . is cooperating with a primary employer and taking his work and doing the work which he is unable to do because of a strike.[5]

---

[3] *Id.* at 676.

[4] *Id.* at 677.

[5] 95 Cong. Rec. 8709 (1949).

This primary decision served only to plant the seed that has developed into what is today recognized as the ally doctrine. In answering the fundamental question that gives rise to the ally exceptions, the court created and left unanswered many important questions. In dealing with these questions, the Board and courts have succeeded in clarifying many issues, but the scope of the ally doctrine remains somewhat clouded.

The subsequent case law on the ally doctrine falls into two general areas—farmed-out struck work and common control. Cases dealing with elements of common control follow either the straight line operation or the co-employer theory of alliance.

FARMED-OUT STRUCK WORK

For a period of several years there were no significant developments regarding the ally doctrine and the performance of struck work. The questions raised by the *Metropolitan Architects* case went unattended. Who has the burden of proving the existence of an ally relationship and how can that burden be met? Must the secondary employer have actual knowledge of the existence of a strike between the union and the primary employer? What is struck work. The answers to these questions slowly began to flow out of the Board and courts in 1955.

Business Machines Board Local 459 (Royal Typewriter)[6] established that the burden of proof is upon the union to show the existence of an ally relationship as an affirmative defense which would remove the secondary employer from the protection of section 8(b)(4) of the Act. The Board went on to hold, however, that the union had failed to show the existence of such special circumstances and that therefore the union's activity constituted a secondary boycott. Although the Second Circuit Court of Appeals agreed with the Board in holding that the union must prove an alliance, it refused enforcement and reversed the NLRB order when it held that the union's proof met the burden established by the Board.

The Royal Typewriter Company was struck by its service personnel. Royal had several different arrangements with customers whereby it was obliged to service and repair their machines. In order to meet these obligations Royal instructed its customers to have the repairs done elsewhere, pay the charges, and send the paid bills to Royal for a refund. However, most customers merely sent

---

[6] 111 N.L.R.B. 317 (1955), *enforcement denied*, 228 F.2d 553 (2d Cir. 1955).

the unpaid bills to Royal who then paid the independent company directly. As a result of these circumstances, the union picketed two of these independents.

Both the NLRB and the Second Circuit Court agreed that the union must prove that the secondary employer was an ally employer. However, they differed as to whether the union had succeeded in meeting that burden. The Board majority agreed with the Trial Examiner who reasoned that since there had been no direct arrangement between Royal and the independents, no alliance was present. The NLRB supported this reasoning by urging the protection of the interests of neutral independents as well as the interests of customers of the primary employer.

The Second Circuit Court of Appeals agreed with dissenting Board Member Peterson in holding that an ally relationship did exist. The court held that the independents were performing struck work and were therefore allies of the primary employer whether or not there was a direct arrangement between Royal and the other employers. The court stated that the employers could have extricated themselves from the dispute by refusing to do the struck work, and that the interests of the striking union are greater than those of either the customers of the primary employer or of the secondary employers. Furthermore,

> . . . an employer is not within the protection of section 8(b)(4)(A) when he knowingly does work which would otherwise be done by the striking employees of the primary employer and where this work is paid for by the primary employer persuant to an arrangement devised and originated by him to enable him to meet his contractual obligations. The result must be the same whether or not the primary employer makes any direct arrangements with the employers providing the services.[7]

It was here established that the union has the burden of proving the existence of an ally relationship.[8] The NLRB and the court took completely opposite positions on the same set of facts. The determination here seemed to turn on whether the independents had knowledge that they were performing struck work. The court's decision holds that there is no requirement for actual knowledge since the parties had constructive knowledge or reason to believe that they were performing struck work.

---

[7] 228 F.2d at 559.

[8] *See also* Teamsters Local 135 (Marsh Foodliners, Inc.), 114 N.L.R.B. 639 (1955); Plumbing and Pipefitting Local 35 (Richard E. Buettner), 126 N.L.R.B. 708 (1960).

A case may arise where the ally employer is unable to determine that the work he is doing is "farmed out". We need not decide whether the picketing of such an employer would be lawful for that is not the situation here. The existence of the strike, the receipt of checks from Royal, and the picketing itself certainly put the independents on notice that some of the work they were doing might be work farmed out by Royal.[9]

The court reasoned that the independents were allies since they had constructive knowledge that they were acting as strikebreakers by performing struck work. The court's failure to define what constitutes sufficient constructive knowledge, however, leaves many important considerations unattended and unanswered.

In *Iron Workers Local 501 (Oliver Whyte Company)*[10] the primary employer had farmed out struck work one week after the strike began. The union's picketing of the ally employer caused a complete shutdown of operations since all means of identifying the struck work had been removed. The Board affirmed the Trial Examiner's decision which held:

> . . . once an employer "allies" himself with the primary employer whose employees are on strike, he stands in the shoes of the primary employer so that the union may lawfully exert the same type of pressure against the former employer as it may against the latter . . . . Moreover, to hold in this case that Respondent could lawfully only induce or encourage the employees to cease work *solely* on the struck-bound work of the Charging Party, would permit the Respondent to perform only a useless and meaningless act because, as the record shows, the employees had no way of knowing whether the orders on which they were working came from the Charging Party or from an employer whose employees were not on strike.[11]

This case is of great significance, for although the Board had recognized the existence of the ally doctrine in previous cases, this is the first case in which the Board actually applied the exception in order to deny a secondary employer the protection of the Act. Of even greater importance, the Board held that under the facts presented in *Whyte*, involving an unidentifiable struck product, the

---

[9] 228 F.2d at 559. *See also* General Drivers and Dairy Employees Local 563 (Fox Valley Material Suppliers Ass'n), 76 N.L.R.B. No. 51, 71 L.R.R.M. 1231, 1235 (1969), where the Board held that the language in *Royal Typewriter* "would seem to impose upon an employer the burden of determining whether or not he is engaged in neutral or ally type work."

[10] 120 N.L.R.B. 856 (1958).

[11] *Id.* at 862.

union may induce and encourage a total refusal to work by the secondary employees. This case established the principle that an ally of the primary employer stands "in the shoes" of the primary employer and is therefore subject to union pressure. In this case the scope of permissible picketing was expanded to encompass the entire operation of the ally because the struck work was not identifiable. Later in the same year the Board ruled that in those circumstances where a struck work alliance exists, but the farmed out work is identifiable, the union may exert pressure to induce or encourage a refusal to handle only such struck work.[12]

These early cases established the basic principles that govern the application of the ally doctrine to farmed out struck work situations. The union has the burden of proof as to the existence of an alliance. The burden is met on a case by case basis depending on the particular facts there presented. In each case, the secondary employer must have actual or constructive knowledge of the existence of a strike and the performance of struck work. An alliance may be terminated by the secondary allied employer by his ceasing to perform farmed out struck work. Struck work is that work which "but for" the strike would be performed by the employees of the primary employer.[13] Finally, the secondary employer stands "in the shoes" of the primary employer in regard to the execution of struck work.[14] In such situations where there is an ally relationship between a primary employer and another employer, the respective interests of secondary employers are lost. Through their own actions in accepting struck work such employers have divested themselves of their neutrality and have lost the protection of section 8(b)(4). However, often the facts are unclear as to whether the secondary employer is accepting struck work and thereby becoming involved in the dispute or is merely engaging in self help in order to expand his business dealings on a permanent basis.

Self Help

In dealing with the ally doctrine, each case seems to turn on the particular facts presented. Different results have been reached on

---

[12] International Die Sinkers Conf. Lodge 410 (General Metals Corp.), 120 N.L.R.B. 1227 (1958).

[13] *See* Chemical Workers Local 36 (Virginia-Carolina Chem. Corp.), 126 N.L.R.B. 905 (1960); Teamsters Local 810 (Fein Can Corp.), 131 N.L.R.B. 59 (1961), *enforced,* 299 F.2d 636 (2d Cir. 1962).

[14] *See* Brewery Workers Local 366 (Adolph Coors Co.), 121 N.L.R.B. 271 (1958), *enforcement denied on other grounds,* 272 F.2d 817 (10th Cir. 1959).

the same facts. It is extremely important therefore to fully understand the facts presented in *National Maritime Local 333 (Picton
and Co.)*[15] where the NLRB held that the secondary employer
was a neutral because the work was undertaken not as struck work
but as a form of self help. The union there was engaged in a
strike against Sabine Towing, a competitor of Picton, and against
Sabine Transport, a competitor of Dixie Carriers, Inc. The union's
picketing activities prevented Picton from performing its towing
services and prevented Dixie from transporting certain barges.
The union claimed that these employers were not protected by
the Act because they had been doing farmed out struck work
and were therefore allies of Sabine.

The Trial Examiner, whose opinion was fully accepted by the
Board, took notice of the following facts in forming the decision.
Picton and Sabine were the only companies doing commercial towing in the area. Almost all their work with various companies was
done on a rotation basis. In the past, if one was unable to perform,
the other would be called to do the task. As a result of the strike
which closed Sabine, Picton was called upon to do all the work.
Picton accepted all the work except that which was contracted to
Sabine while the union picketed only those jobs which it honestly
believed would have been handled by the struck primary employer.
Although the Trial Examiner found that Picton was performing
work which would have been done by Sabine but for the strike,
he ruled that Picton and the customers were not allies of Sabine
and that therefore the union violated the Act by conducting a
secondary boycott.

The Trial Examiner's opinion drew a sharp contrast between the
facts here presented and those of the *Royal Typewriter* case. It
was on the basis of this contrast that he found that the customers
and Picton were not allies, but were neutrals who were merely
engaging in self help.

> Although it would seem clear that Picton and the customers were
> not wholly innocent in the matter in that they clearly knew that
> Picton was performing some work at least that Sabine would
> have performed absent a strike, it would appear that a customer
> arranging for substitute services during a strike does not make
> himself or the substitute an "ally" merely because he knowingly
> arranges for services and the substitute knowingly performs them.
> In the absense of a direct or indirect arrangement by the struck
> employer with the customer or the secondary employer (Picton) to

---

[15] 131 N.L.R.B. 693 (1961).

have the work performed for its account, the secondary employers
do not lose the protection afforded a "neutral" under the Act.[16]

In reaching such decisions, the Board and courts must decide
where to draw the line. A secondary employer can be either a neutral or an ally; he is either protected from secondary boycotts or
he is found to be in the shoes of the primary employer and
susceptible to union pressure. There are no fixed rules governing
this area of law. Each case must therefore be decided on the basis
of the facts presented. A slight change in the facts is often enough
to convert a neutral into an ally. In a case,[17] similar to *Royal
Typewriter* the Board held, with the approval of the District of
Columbia Circuit Court, that

> This privilege of self help, however, is not an unqualified author-
> ization to a secondary employer to perform with its employees the
> struck work of its supplier of services, on the struck employer's
> equipment, and by arrangement with that employer. Texas (the
> secondary employer) could independently have used its own em-
> ployees or the employees of any other employer to load and trans-
> port its fuel without sacrificing its neutrality, so long as this did
> not involve the arranged replacement of Ingram's employees by
> Texas employees to perform the services for which they were
> hired by Ingram.[18]

The case law reveals that the performance of farmed out struck
work divests a secondary of his neutrality, for such action makes
him a part of the primary dispute. Both the NLRB and the courts
recognize that the economic impact of farmed out struck work
is much the same as the hiring of strikebreakers, since the secondary's activity has a direct economic impact on the primary dispute.
It is not always easy to determine whether an ally relationship has
been created by the performance of struck work. The NLRB and
the courts have viewed this problem as a question of fact to be
decided on a case by case basis.

Struck Work

One of the most important and difficult questions of fact facing
the Board and courts is whether the work, knowingly accepted by
arrangement between the primary and the secondary employers,

---

[16] *Id.* at 699.

[17] Masters, Mates, and Pilots Local 28 (Ingram Barge Co.), 136 N.L.R.B.
1175 (1962), *enforced*, 321 F.2d 376 (D.C. Cir. 1963).

[18] 136 N.L.R.B. at 1188.

is struck work—work, which *but for* the strike would be performed by the employees of the primary employer.

In *Woodworkers Local 3-101 (Priest Logging, Inc.)*[19] the Board and the Ninth Circuit Court of Appeals held that the secondary employer may accept work from the primary according to a special arrangement caused by the existence of a strike and still retain a neutral status. In this case, the union was engaged in a strike against Eclipse Lumber Company. Eclipse had arranged and paid for Bayside Log Dump Company to unload and store logs during the strike. Normally this work was done by Eclipse employees. Eclipse had never used the services of Bayside before. Even though the Board agreed with the Trial Examiner that the work done by Bayside duplicated work tasks which the striking employees ordinarily performed, it overturned the examiner's finding of an ally relationship.

> . . . Bayside's services to Eclipse were not "struck work" services. Thus, Bayside's acceptance from Priest of Eclipse logs for temporary storage while Eclipse's operations remained strikebound neither aided Eclipse in the conduct of any business activity constituting the reason for the latter's existence, nor deprived the striking Eclipse employees of any of the work opportunities they were legitimately interested in preserving. . . . For the logs were destined for later delivery to Eclispe when its operations were resumed, and the normal unloading work of the striking employees thus remained to be performed.[20]

On the basis of the facts in this case the Board recognized the work done by Bayside as duplicating rather than supplanting the work done by the primary employer's employees. The neutrality of secondary parties is not easily overcome. It is the policy of the Act to protect employers from direct envolvement in disputes that are not their own. Under the ally doctrine, only when the work performed by the secondary employer is struck work does the secondary lose his neutral status.

> Such services in a sense tend to help the primary employer and to diminish the economic impact of a strike. Nevertheless, those services should not be held to remove the independent contractors from the protection of the secondary boycott provision of the National Labor Relations Act unless the services supplant the work of the striking employees with the purpose and effect of enabling

---

[19] 137 N.L.R.B. 352 (1962), *enforced*, 319 F.2d 655 (9th Cir. 1963).

[20] 137 N.L.R.B. at 354.

the primary employer to carry on its usual operations during and notwithstanding the strike.[21]

The *Priest Logging* case established a very important principle. The ally doctrine does not encompass every instance of work done by secondary employers during a strike. Work that merely duplicates the work that will subsequently be done by the striking employees is not struck work. This decision maintains the balance between the competing interests of unions and neutral secondary parties. The ruling here prevents an overly broad application of the ally doctrine in a manner that would ignore the legitimate interests of secondary parties. To ignore these interests would allow the unions to conduct a secondary boycott in violation of the Act.[22]

The NLRB relied on this same reasoning in *Teamsters Local 868 (Mercer Storage Co.)*[23] in order to prevent an unnecessarily broad application of the ally doctrine. In cases involving alleged ally situations it is necessary therefore to consider the impact of the tasks being performed by the secondary employer in order to determine whether he has lost or retained his status as a neutral.[24]

Often the determination that the work being done by the secondary employer is struck work depends on other factual considera-

---

[21] 319 F.2d at 657.

[22] *See* Madden v. Teamsters Local 810, 222 F. Supp. 635 (N.D. Ill. 1963), in which an ally relationship was held to exist where the actions of the secondary could not have affected work normally done by the striking employees.

[23] 156 N.L.R.B. 67, 70 (1965). The Board stated:

It is true that Mercer's business with Mid-County increased as a result of the strike, and that Mercer was handling cars for Mid-County which would not have gone to Mercer's premises but for the strike. But this is not enough to invoke the "ally" doctrine . . . . The "ally" doctrine may be invoked where an otherwise neutral employer "knowingly does work which would otherwise be done by the striking employees." . . . But in the instant case the striking employees were salesmen, and none of their work was performed at Mercer's warehouse or by Mercer employees . . . . To be sure, the purpose and effect of storing Mid-County's cars at Mercer was to avoid the impact of the lawful picketing at Mid-County and assist the latter in combatting the strike. But under the present statute, as authoritatively construed, these considerations do not amount to legal justification for involving the neutral employer in a labor controversy to which he is otherwise a stranger.

[24] *See* Chemical Workers Local 61 (Sterling Drug, Inc.), 189 N.L.R.B. No. 111, 76 L.R.R.M. 1508 (1971), in which the secondary employer was found to be a neutral because the work it performed for the primary employer did not supplant the work of the striking employees.

tions. In those cases where there is an agreement which was made before the commencement of the strike, the relevant factual inquiry has to do with the motivation of the primary employer.

Preexisting Agreements

As shown in *Brewery Workers Local 8 (Bert P. Williams, Inc.)*,[25] the determination of the ally issue depends on the facts and how they are interpreted by the Board. In this case, the Trial Examiner had found that the secondary was not an ally of the struck employer. The Board majority reversed this holding. The facts presented leave much room for doubt. O'Brien Distributors, Inc. had entered a collective bargaining contract with the union. This contract expired March 1, 1963. On December 27, 1962, O'Brien gave the union notice that it might discontinue delivery operations and contract out the work, and O'Brien began negotiations with Bert P. Williams for a delivery contract. On February 28, 1963 the union's strike began. On the same date O'Brien reached a verbal agreement with Williams to conduct the delivery work. Williams began delivery work on the fourth of March and a contract was signed on the seventh. The Board majority reversed the Trial Examiner and held that Williams was an ally of O'Brien within the meaning set forth in *Royal Typewriter*.

> It may be, of course, that sometime in the future O'Brien might have contracted out its delivery work, but the decision to contract out coincidentally with the strike was, we hold, caused by the failure or imminent failure of collective bargaining negotiations with Respondent and represented an attempt by O'Brien to insure continuance of beer deliveries notwithstanding the strike by its own employees.[26]

This decision is not entirely supported by the facts. The Board ignored much in deciding that the subcontract was a ploy to avoid the economic consequence of a strike. Certain of the facts presented here do support the Board's view, but the position taken by the Trial Examiner and dissenting Member Leedom seems to be more strongly supported by the facts and by policy considerations. The neutral status of secondary employers should not be overcome unless the facts present at least substantial reason to believe that the actions were undertaken to avoid the consequences of a strike.

---

[25] 148 N.L.R.B. 728 (1964).

[26] *Id.* at 733.

The dissent took the position that the agreement between O'Brien
and Williams was not struck work which would have been performed by the striking employees but for the strike, but was work
which would have been subcontracted even if the strike had not
occurred.

> Admittedly, O'Brien knew on February 28, that O'Brien employees
> would not report for work upon expiration of the contract, but it
> does not follow from this, in view of all the circumstances, including
> the negotiations with Williams, that O'Brien subcontracted the work
> because the employees decided to strike. The foregoing makes clear,
> as it did to the Trial Examiner, that O'Brien subcontracted the
> work, not by reason of the strike, but because O'Brien was able to
> make economically suitable terms with Williams but could not do so
> with the union.[27]

Even though the facts do not entirely support the result reached
in *Williams*, the law governing the status of secondary employers
is equitable. Even where there is a subcontracting agreement in
existence before the strike, the case law has established that

> . . . a secondary employer is not protected against . . . picketing
> under the following circumstances:
> (1) When he "knowingly" does work that would have been per-
> formed by employees of the striking employer if the strike had not
> occurred, and
> (2) when the "struck work" is paid for by the struck employer
> "persuant to an arrangement devised and originated by him to
> enable him to meet his contractual obligations." [28]

As can be clearly seen, the rules of the *Royal Typewriter* and
Metropolitan Architects cases have remained intact. A secondary
employer is divested of his neutral status upon his becoming an
ally of the primary employer. However, certain safeguards also
exist to protect the neutrality of secondary parties. The Board
stated that

> . . . an employer is not deprived of his status as a "neutral" and
> made a party to a primary dispute between himself and the union,
> within the meaning of Section 8(b)(4), by the mere fact that he
> persists in doing business with an employer who is involved in
> such a dispute. Nor is an employer deprived of his status as a

---

[27] *Id.* at 736-7.

[28] Warehouse Union Local 6 (Hershey Chocolate Corp.), 153 N.L.R.B. 1051,
1062 (1965), *enforced*, 378 F.2d 1 (9th Cir. 1967).

"neutral" because his business dealings have themselves created the condition giving rise to the dispute.[29]

Reestablishment of Neutral Status

It has been recognized by the NLRB and the Courts that a secondary employer may reestablish his neutrality by relinquishing his performance of struck work.[30] While the more recent case of *Laundry Workers (Morrison's of San Diego, Inc.)*[31] affirmed this principle, it also presented the NLRB with a complicated fact situation that caused further consideration of this rule of law. The union had requested that Morrison's cease the performance of certain struck work. Morrison's failed to respond to this request. The union therefore commenced to picket Morrison's as an ally of the primary employer being unaware that all struck work had been stopped before the picketing began. Upon learning of Morrison's actions, the union immediately withdrew the pickets. The Trial Examiner held that the union had violated the Act because Morrison's was a neutral employer who was under no duty to inform the union when it terminated the struck work. The NLRB reversed this holding.

> In our opinion, to give affect to both these distinctions (between allies and neutrals) and the accomodation which must be maintained between the competing interests underlying Section 8(b)(4) (B) of the Act, the ally, in order to expunge its identity with the primary dispute, is under an affirmative duty to notify the picketing union that struck work shall no longer be performed.[32]

This holding does not disturb the rule that an ally may terminate his involvement in the primary dispute by ceasing to handle struck work.[33] It merely states that where, as here, the union could not ordinarily discover that the secondary employer had ceased being an ally, the secondary employer had a duty to so inform. This requirement, like most others applicable to farmed out struck work, depends on findings of fact, which should be made in a

---

[29] 153 N.L.R.B. at 1064.

[30] NLRB v. Business Machine Board 459, 228 F.2d 553 (2d Cir. 1955).

[31] 164 N.L.R.B. 426 (1967).

[32] *Id.* at 427.

[33] *See* Service Employees Local 250 (Independent Acceptance Co.), 187 N.L.R.B. No. 28, 76 L.R.R.M. 1860 (1970).

realistic, nonmechanical manner that avoids reliance upon rigid rules.

The NLRB and the courts have dealt with the doctrine that originated in the *Metropolitan Architects* case in a piecemeal fashion. The farmed out struck work case law seems on the whole to accomodate successfully the statutory proscriptions on secondary boycotts and the guarantees of primary union activity. However, the rules leave the NLRB and the courts a great deal of freedom in applying the law and in interpreting the facts of each case in terms of the legal requirements. In dealing with struck work situations, the case law reveals a fairly uniform body of law that has been applied in a reasonably equitable manner. The differences of opinion between the Board and the Second Circuit Court of Appeals have been resolved gradually. On the other hand, even this degree of uniformity and clarity in the case law has not developed in regard to those areas of the ally doctrine dealing with elements of common control. The NLRB and the courts have encountered serious difficulties in dealing with this area.

ELEMENTS OF COMMON CONTROL

Unlike the struck work cases, which did not begin to answer the questions created in *Metropolitan Architects* for a number of years, there was an immediate reaction to the elements of common control presented in that case. The initial line of cases found an ally relationship because of the existence of common ownership or of a straight line operation. Out of these earlier standards developed the second type of common control alliance—the co-employer. The developments of both concepts were characterized by serious disagreements between the Board and the circuit courts. Some of these conflicts still remain controversial issues, and make the administration of this area of labor law one that is characterized by frequent litigation and unsettled law.

Early Case Law and Conflict

The *National Union of Maritime Cooks (Irwin-Lyons Lumber Co.)* case [34] was the first in which elements of common ownership and control were used as the basis for divesting an employer of his neutrality and for finding the existence of an ally relationship.

---

[34] 87 N.L.R.B. 54 (1949).

> The Trial Examiner found that the Coos River Boom Company
> is engaged as a public utility . . . in the transportation of logs;
> that Irwin-Lyons Lumber Company is a separate corporate entity
> engaged in logging and sawmill operations; that the stock owner-
> ship and managerial control in the Coos River Boom Company and
> in the Irwin-Lyons Lumber Company are vested, substantially, in
> the same individuals; and that both companies are, in effect,
> engaged in "one straight line operation," i.e. the Lumber Company
> cuts the logs, the Boom Company transports the logs down the
> river, and the Lumber Company saws the logs into lumber at the
> mill. On the basis of these facts, we agree with the Trial Examiner
> that the Boom Company is not a neutral or wholly unconcerned
> employer, within the meaning of Section 8(b)(4)(A) of the
> Act.[35]

The Board's finding of a straight line operation was based upon
common ownership, common management control, and a community
of operations.

United Carpenters and Joiners (J. G. Roy and Sons)[36] presented
certain elements of common ownership and control that were similar to *Irwin-Lyons.* The NLRB held that the employers were engaged in a straight line operation. The First Circuit Court of
Appeals, however, rejected the Board's view of *Irwin-Lyons.*

The pertinent facts were that the union was involved in a dispute with Roy Lumber Company. In furtherance of that dispute
the union picketed Roy Construction Company. The union defended
this activity on the grounds that the Construction Company was
an ally under *Irwin-Lyons.* The NLRB agreed with this conten-
tion for there was common ownership and because "Roy Lumber
was Roy Construction's sole source of supply of millwork lumber."[37] The Board found neither common management control
nor a community of operation. Member Rodgers dissented on this
basis.

The Circuit Court agreed with the dissenting Board member in
holding that there was no straight line operation here. The NLRB
had ignored many significant facts in concluding that the two
enterprises were, in reality, one straight line operation. None of
the five Roy Brothers was an official or an employee of both companies. While all five brothers were on the board of directors of
Roy Construction and four were on the board of the Lumber

[35] *Id.* at 56.

[36] 118 N.L.R.B. 286 (1957), *enforcement denied,* 251 F.2d 771 (1st Cir. 1958).

[37] 118 N.L.R.B. at 287.

Company, neither board exercised management control. The Construction company's purchases from Roy Lumber amounted to only five percent of that company's annual sales. The court held that there was no "unified production effort" as in *Irwin-Lyons* and that there "must be more than the potential control inherent in common ownership" [38] in order to establish the existence of a straight line operation. Common ownership and common control were necessary to establish an ally relationship. [39]

The NLRB position allowed a neutral secondary employer to be reached solely on the grounds of common ownership. Such a position does not protect the interests of a truly neutral employer. Common ownership alone does not establish that the two entities were acting as one to overcome the effects of the labor dispute with the union.

The Board continued to follow this position in *Warehouse Workers Local 688 (Bachman Machine Co.).* [40] In this case the union picketed Bachman in furtherance of its strike against Plastics Molding Company. The two companies were commonly owned and the same individual served as president of both corporations. The Board found that the element of common ownership was clearly present and that there was also common control because the individual who was president of both companies participated in negotiations with the union.

The Eighth Circuit Court of Appeals overturned the Board order and remanded the case to the NLRB. [41] The court held that the president of both companies participated in the negotiations as the president of Plastics and dealt only with the union representing Plastics employees. This activity had nothing to do with Bachman and its employees and was therefore insufficient to establish common management control.

On remand, the Board declared that it would "treat the court's opinion as the law establishing this case." [42] The conflicting views of the NLRB and the circuit courts were put to rest in this case. Common ownership and common control are necessary to establish

---

[38] 251 F.2d at 773.

[39] Teamsters Local 249 (Polar Water Co.), 120 N.L.R.B. 155 (1958).

[40] 121 N.L.R.B. 1229 (1958), *rev'd and remanded,* 266 F.2d 599 (8th Cir. 1959).

[41] 266 F.2d 599.

[42] Warehouse Workers Local 688 (Bachman Machine Co.), 121 N.L.R.B. 743, 744 (1959).

the existence of an ally relationship. However, the law was not yet settled as to what constitutes a sufficient community of interest and control to establish a straight line operation.

Straight Line Operations and Community of Interests

Although certain conflicts between the Board and circuit courts had been worked out, the Board itself was not in complete agreement as to the degree of common control and ownership required to divest an employer of his neutrality. The case of *Teamsters Local 282 (Acme Concrete and Supply Corp.)*[43] involved a complicated fact situation. The union was engaged in a dispute with Twin County Transit Mix Inc., a producer, seller and distributor of concrete. The premises occupied by Twin were owned and shared by Acme, which sells sand, gravel, and other material used in ready mix concrete. Twin purchased ninety-nine percent of its supplies from Acme which amounted to eighty-five percent of Acme sales. The sole stockholder of Acme was the wife of Twin's general manager. The actual operation of Acme was in the charge of the Twin general manager's two brothers. Two unsecured loans had been made by Acme to Twin. In addition Twin paid no rent for its use of the premises owned by Acme. The Board concluded that there was an ally relationship between Twin and Acme and that therefore the union did not violate the Act by picketing the entire premises occupied by Twin and Acme.

> We need not here determine whether the relationship between Acme and Twin County is one of "single employer" or "ally." It is sufficient that Acme and Twin County have such identity and community of interests as negative the claim that Acme is a neutral employer. This is established by the facts found above relating to the interrelationship and interdependence of the two companies, and to the close family connections among those who have important roles in the operations of both companies. Accordingly, as Acme is not the kind of third person who was intended to be protected by Section 8(b)(4), . . . we shall dismiss the complaint.[44]

The Board's decision here represents a significant expansion of the single employer or ally concept. This expansion of the standards was unacceptable to Member Rodgers, who criticized the Board for equating "family connections" with common ownership and control in his dissent. The facts show that the two companies

---

[43] 137 N.L.R.B. 1321 (1962).

[44] *Id.* at 1324.

were separately owned despite the close family connections. Member Rodgers felt that the close business relations here could not be characterized as any more than "doing business." In his view the companies were separate legal entities, separately owned, and separately managed. Member Rodgers felt that the Board had gone beyond its *J. G. Roy and Sons* decision and had found an alliance where there was no evidence supporting such a conclusion:

> . . . there are a number of factors to be weighed when determining whether or not such a relationship exists, such factors at the very least being common ownership, common management, common control of labor relations, intergration of operations, and complete dependence of one company on the other. These factors are patently missing from this case.[45]

The great danger in the NLRB position taken here is that the finding of an alliance rests, at least in part, on what the Board characterized as close business ties and which could also be described as "doing business." The secondary boycott ban loses all meaning when an ally relationship is found on the basis of "doing business." Even though this case involves an unusually high degree of interrelationship and interdependence, the Board's opinion comes dangerously close to finding an alliance because one firm has done business with a struck employer. The statute seeks to protect neutrals from disputes of others. In order to foster this policy, the Board should follow more decisive and demanding standards similar to those suggested by the late Mr. Rodgers. Such a policy preserves the vitality of section 8(b)(4)(B) and provides a means for attaining greater stability in industrial relations.

Co-Ownership

Even where there is extensive co-ownership the Board has held that an employer may remain neutral to the labor disputes of a commonly owned business enterprise. The Board has held that

> Common ownership alone is not sufficient. There must be in addition such actual or active common control, as distinguished from merely a potential, as to denote an appreciable integration of operations and management policies.[46]

---

[45] *Id.* at 1325-6.

[46] Teamsters Local 639 (Poole's Warehousing, Inc.), 158 N.L.R.B. 1281, 1286 (1966).

Printing Pressmen Local 46 (Knight Newspapers, Inc.)[47] is
illustrative of the considerations involved in such matters. A
Detroit and a Miami newspaper were both owned by the same
Ohio corporation. The union was engaged in a dispute with the
Miami paper and picketed the Detroit Free Press in furtherance
of that strike. The Board upheld the neutrality of the secondary
employer stating that without the exercise of common control
there is no basis for divesting the commonly owned secondary employer of its neutrality.

To impose an ally relation in this factual setting would create
a fiction based on the mere potential ability to exercise common
management control. The Board has opposed this reasoning and
has protected the neutrality of secondary employers where there
is extensive common ownership but no active common control.[48]

Because the ally doctrine is an exception to the general rule
contained in section 8(b)(4) prohibiting secondary activity, it
should be applied only in those situations where there is an un-
questionable loss of neutrality and involvement in the dispute between primary parties. The NLRB and courts have encountered
considerable conflict over what circumstances convert a neutral
independent contractor into a co-employer ally.

Co-Employer

The NLRB positions regarding independent contractors has been
that an independent employer could not loose his status as a neutral without actual proof of common ownership and control.[49] This
view follows that set forth by the Supreme Court in *NLRB v.
Denver Building and Construction Trades Council.*[50]

> We agree with the Board . . . in its conclusion that the fact that the
> contractor and subcontractor were engaged in the same construction
> projects, and that the contractors had some supervision over the

---

[47] 138 N.L.R.B. 1346 (1962), *enforced*, 322 F.2d 405 (D.C. Cir. 1963).

[48] *See also* Los Angeles Newspaper Guild Local 69 (Hearst Corp.), 185
N.L.R.B. No. 25, 75 L.R.R.M. 1014 (1970); AFTRA Washington-Baltimore
Local (Hearst Corp.), 185 N.L.R.B. No. 26, 75 L.R.R.M. 1018 (1970).

[49] *See* Teamsters Local 20 (National Cement Prod. Co.), 115 N.L.R.B. 1290
(1956); Truck Drivers Local 728 (Empire State Express, Inc.), 116 N.L.R.B.
615 (1956), both denying the existence of an allied co-employer relationship.
See also Truck Drivers Local 107 (Sterling Wire Prod. Co.), 137 N.L.R.B.
1330 (1962), where the Board found that the employer was not a neutral
but was a co-employer who was not protected from the union's lawful
primary picketing activity.

[50] 341 U.S. 675 (1951).

subcontractors work did not eliminate the status of each as an independent contractor or make the employees of one the employees of the other. The business relationship between independent contractors is too well established in law to be overridden without clear language doing so.[51]

This language does not apply to the ally doctrine in a manner that procludes an independent contractor, under the proper circumstances, from also being a co-employer. Rather this language means that the neutrality of an independent contractor can only be overcome by clear and convincing proof.

Teamsters Local 24 (A.C.E. Transportation Co.)[52] was the first in a line of cases in which the Board and the District of Columbia Circuit Court of Appeals disagreed over fundamental principles. In that case the union had a dispute with the lessor of trucking equipment. In furtherance of this dispute the union picketed the trucking terminal of A.C.E., a lessee, and induced A.C.E. employees to cease work. A.C.E. trucks were operated by the employees of the lessor. The Trial Examiner had held that A.C.E. and the lessor were co-employers and that therefore the union's activity did not constitute a violation of the Act. The NLRB overruled this decision. The Board majority held that

> The Supreme Court's and the Board's criteria for determining the existence of an "independent contractor" relationship requires consideration of "the total situation, including the risk undertaken, the control exercised, the opportunity for profit from sound management. . . ." The control exercised by the lessee over the manner in which the work was done by the employees of the lessors cannot be solely determinative of the status of "independent contractor," nor make the employees of a private contractor the employees of the person with whom he contracts concerning their service.[53]

After reviewing the facts presented here in terms of the standards enunciated above, the Board concluded that there was no co-employer status here involved. The union's activity in picketing the lessee was a violation of the Act.

> In view of the legislative background and purposes of Section 8(b)(4), the Board has consistently considered that an employer is not deprived of his status as a "neutral" and made a party to a

[51] *Id.* at 689-90.

[52] 120 N.L.R.B. 1103 (1958), *enforcement denied*, 266 F.2d 675 (D.C. Cir. 1959).

[53] 120 N.L.R.B. at 1107.

primary dispute between himself and the union, within the meaning of Section (8) (b) (4) (A), by the mere fact that he persists in doing business with an employer who is involved in such a dispute. . . . Nor is an employer deprived of his status as a "neutral" because his business dealings have themselves created the condition giving rise to the dispute. Nor by the fact he has control over the employees of another employer, in the manner in which they perform their work for him.[54]

The NLRB decision was based on a consideration of all significant facts that would tend to indicate the existence of a co-employer relationship. The Board utilized specific standards in reaching its determination that the lessees had remained neutral. Although the application of determinative standards may introduce a degree of rigidity, it appears that this was minimal. In addition, the use of these standards allows the parties to a dispute to determine for themselves what the boundaries of that dispute are.

In overruling the NLRB, the District of Columbia Court chose to look at the total fabric and setting of the strike and picketing:

> The answer to the problem before us cannot be reached by the use of any legalistic word or phrase, such as "co-employer" or "independent contractor," or even "ally." It cannot be solved by the strict application of the technicalities which adhere to such legal terms. The problem is, as dissenting Member Bean put it, whether the facts or circumstances are such that the strikers violated the secondary boycott provision of the statute when they picketed the terminals of ACE and induced the employees of ACE to honor their picket line.[55]

The court concluded that A.C.E. was not a neutral because, "the many tiny strands of ACE control over these drivers cannot be extricated from the total fabric of mutual obligation."[56] Such a view sets no clear standard from which the disputing parties can guide their conduct. The lack of clarity and the reliance on "tiny strands" of control actually discourages, rather than encourages industrial peace and undermines the policy of the Act.[57] It benefits

---

[54] *Id.* at 1109.

[55] 266 F.2d at 680.

[56] *Id.*

[57] *See* Building Service Employees Local 32-J (Terminal Barber Shops), 135 N.L.R.B. 909 (1962), *enforcement denied,* 313 F.2d 880 (D.C. Cir. 1963), in which the Board and the District of Columbia Court took the same respective positions. *See also* Carpet Layers Local 419 (Sears, Roebuck and Co.), 176 N.L.R.B. No. 120, 71 L.R.R.M. 1372 (1969), *order modified*

unions as well as neutral secondary employers to know what are the permissible boundaries of strike and picketing activity under section 8(b)(4)(B). The court position serves further to confuse an already difficult issue. The ban on secondary boycotts is based on the protection of two equally fundamental interests. The facts of any case must be reviewed with the goal of balancing the competing interests of unions and secondary employers. While neither of these can be fully protected neither should they be easily overcome.

CONCLUDING REMARKS

The secondary boycott provision of the Act has an underlying policy of balancing the protection afforded to unions and neutral secondary employers. The ally doctrine constitutes an exception to the proscription of section 8(b)(4)(B). This exception works to divest secondary employers of their neutrality and thereby makes them a party to the primary dispute. This exception has been applied to several circumstances each of which presents special considerations for the National Labor Relations Board and the courts. In dealing with each area—farmed out struck work, straight line operations, and co-employers—the Board and courts have proceeded on a case by case basis that relies heavily on the facts of each case. In general the case law has established that a secondary employer loses his neutrality and becomes an ally in the primary dispute: when he aids an employer in his dispute with a union by doing struck work, when the operations of the primary and secondary employers are commonly owned and controlled, and when there is a highly integrated community of interests between the primary and secondary employers.

This approach has placed a tremendous amount of discretion in the hands of the NLRB and the courts. In each area there are conflicts between Board and court decisions. These conflicts undermine the clear and predictable administration of the Act, particularly as in the *A.C.E.* case where the District of Columbia Circuit Court seemed to be evolving a doctrine that greatly expanded union rights at the expense of the neutral employer.

---

and case remanded, 429 F.2d 747 (D.C. Cir. 1970), *on remand,* 190 N.L.R.B. No. 28, 77 L.R.R.M. 1060 (1971).

CHAPTER IV

Consumer Boycotts

Section 8(b) (4) (i) (ii) (B)[1] of the National Labor Relations Act, as amended, pertains to the right of a labor union having a dispute with one employer to picket the premises of a secondary employer who deals in, or utilizes the product or service of, the primary employer. This so-called secondary boycott provision states that:

> It shall be an unfair labor practice for a labor organization or its agents—
> (4) (i) to engage in, or to induce or encourage any individual employed by any person engaged in commerce or in an industry affecting commerce to engage in, a strike or a refusal in the course of his employment to use, manufacture, process, transport, or otherwise handle or work on any goods, articles, materials, or commodities or to perform any services; or (ii) to threaten, coerce, or restrain any person engaged in commerce or in an industry affecting commerce, where in either case an object thereof is—
> (B) forcing or requiring any person to cease using, selling, handling, transporting, or otherwise dealing in the products of any other producer, processor, or manufacturer, or to cease doing business with any other person. . . . *Provided further,* That for the purposes of this paragraph (4) only, nothing contained in such paragraph shall be construed to prohibit publicity, other than picketing, for the purpose of truthfully advising the public, including consumers . . . , that a product or products are produced by an employer with whom the labor organization has a primary dispute and are distributed by another employer. . . .[2]

Section 8(b) (4) (i) (B) applies to the encouragement or inducement of *employees* to engage in certain activity for the objectives listed in the statute. Violations of this provision frequently occur in cases where employees of a neutral employer are used as an indirect means of exerting economic pressure upon the primary employer. On the other hand, section 8(b) (4) (ii) (B) involves union activity that is directed at *any person engaged in commerce,*

---

[1] Labor Management Reporting and Disclosure Act of 1959, § 704, 29 U.S.C. § 158 (b) (4) (i) (ii) (B).

[2] *Id.*

usually the neutral secondary employer, as a means of achieving the objectives prohibited by the Act in subsection B. Although violations of this latter section take many forms, one of the more common and controversial is the consumer boycott. This chapter deals with the legal and practical implications of consumer picketing secondary boycotts under section 8(b)(4)(ii)(B).

Consumer boycotts most often take the form of appeals to the consuming public not to purchase a product produced by the primary employer and merchandised by the neutral secondary employer. These appeals take place upon the premises of the secondary employer and generally involve picketing activity. The publicity proviso found in section 8(b)(4)(B) is applied to determine the legality of the union's actions, only when activity *"other than picketing"* is utilized, such as the process of handbilling.

A literal reading of the statutory language clearly prohibits all secondary consumer boycotts when exercised by means of picketing. This prohibition is made especially clear by the publicity proviso, which creates a limited exception for all forms of publicity other than picketing. It shall be pointed out that the congressional intent was to outlaw secondary boycotts that exert pressure on a neutral employer by persuading customers of that employer to cease doing business with him.[3] The secondary boycott provisions, as amended in 1959, were intended to tighten this prohibition against all secondary boycotts. The legislative history of the Landrum-Griffin Act clearly illustrates that Congress intended to eliminate consumer picketing secondary boycotts.[4]

Pursuant to these mandates the NLRB made several determinations prohibiting all secondary consumer picketing.[5] Unfortunately, after section 8(b)(4)(ii)(B) had been in effect for five years, the Supreme Court reversed the Board's position and allowed certain types of consumer picketing.[6] The effect of this, the *Tree Fruits* doctrine, was to expand the scope of a union's dispute with

---

[3] 2 NLRB, Legislative History of the Labor-Management Reporting and Disclosure Act of 1959 at 1615 (1959) [hereinafter cited as 2 Legis. Hist.].

[4] 2 Legis. Hist. at 1615.

[5] *See* United Wholesale Employees Local 261 (Perfection Mattress and Spring Co.), 129 N.L.R.B. 1014 (1960); Fruit and Vegetable Packers Local 760 (Tree Fruits Labor Relations Committee), 132 N.L.R.B. 1172 (1961); Upholsterers Twin City Local 61 (Minneapolis House Furnishings Co.), 132 N.L.R.B. 40 (1961).

[6] NLRB v. Fruit and Vegetable Packers Local 760 (Tree Fruits Labor Relations Committee), 377 U.S. 58 (1964).

a primary employer. The manner of this extension was to allow for picketing at premises that were not part of the primary situs of the dispute. Neutral secondary employers were exposed to union pressure that the Act had been intended to prohibit and that the NLRB had initially held illegal. Additionally, the doctrine has subsequently been applied in a wide variety of cases involving important variations of the facts presented in *Tree Fruits*. This has had the effect of extending the doctrine even beyond the scope of the Supreme Court's original decision.

It is the thesis of this chapter that the Supreme Court's *Tree Fruits* decision planted the seeds of labor relations instability in this area of secondary boycotts. While the *Tree Fruits* decision itself is, at best, questionable, the more significant problem lies in recent NLRB applications of the doctrine. An overly broad interpretation of *Tree Fruits* creates an undesirable imbalance in favor of a union's right to publicize a dispute and in total disregard of a neutral employer's right to be protected.

To determine the causes and extent of this imbalance and to facilitate the search for a solution, it will be necessary to first review the early NLRB decisions. Following an examination of the facts and decision in *Tree Fruits,* an analysis of recent court and Board decisions will be undertaken.

EARLY DECISIONS UNDER LANDRUM-GRIFFIN

The early decisions of the NLRB under the 1959 Landrum-Griffin Amendments reveal an adherence to the statutory scheme of balancing union and neutral interests. Neutral secondary employers were protected by NLRB enforcement of the statutory prohibition of consumer directed appeals by picketing. On the other hand, the rights of unions to publicize labor disputes were protected under the publicity proviso where means other than picketing had been employed.

Consumer Directed Picketing

The NLRB position on consumer boycotts accompanied by picketing activity was clearly stated in *United Wholesale Employees Local 261 (Perfection Mattress and Spring Co.).*[7] Here, the union conducted consumer picketing at retail department stores which were customers of the primary employer, Perfection Mattress.

---

[7] 129 N.L.R.B. 1014 (1960), *enforced,* 321 F.2d 612 (5th Cir. 1963).

During the fourteen days of picketing activity, no deliveries to the secondary employers were stopped, no neutral employee quit or refused to work, and no retail department store employees refused to handle Perfection goods. The picketing was conducted after the retail department store employees arrived at work and before they left the stores. The union picketed at entrances used by the public and by employees. The picket signs were addressed to the consuming public and stated that products made by Perfection Mattress and Spring Company were produced by non-union labor and urged consumers not to buy them. Based on these facts, the NLRB concluded that under section 8(b) (4) (ii) (B) the union had engaged in prohibited secondary activity by coercing or restraining any person engaged in commerce" where "an object thereof is . . ., forcing or requiring any person to cease using, selling, handling . . . or otherwise dealing in the products of any other producer."

Examining the legislative history of the Act, the Board made specific reference to the remarks of the then Congressman (now Senator) Griffin, a co-sponsor of the new bill:

> Mr. Griffin: Then we are not talking about picketing at the place of the primary dispute. We are concerned about picketing at the store where the furniture is sold. Under the present law, if picketing happens to be at the employee entrance so that clearly the purpose of the picketing is to induce the employees of the secondary employer not to handle the products of the primary employer, the boycott could be enjoined.
>
> However if the picketing happened to be around at the consumer entrance, and if the purpose of the picketing were to coerce the employer not to handle those goods, then under the present law, because of technical interpretations, the boycott would not be covered.
>
> Mr. Brown of Ohio: In other words, the Taft-Hartley Act does not cover such a situation now . . . (b)ut the Griffin-Landrum Bill would?
>
> Mr. Griffin: Our bill would; that is right. If the purpose of the picketing is to coerce or to restrain the employer of that second establishment, to get him not to do business with the manufacturer —then such a boycott could be stopped.[8]

By its reference to this language, the Board clearly illustrated the specific application of the amended statute to this case. It was concluded that the Act clearly prohibited secondary consumer picketing, a conclusion strongly supported by the actual language of the 1959 amendments as well as the accompanying legislative history.

---

[8] 129 N.L.R.B. 1014, 1022 n.17; 2 Legis. Hist. at 1615.

The Board members went on to consider the relationship of the publicity proviso to the facts presented in *Perfection Mattress*. It was concluded that although the publicity proviso was intended to exempt certain activity from the proscription of section 8(b) (4)(B), secondary consumer picketing was not among these.

> Moreover, although the new section contains a proviso which exempts certain conduct engaged in "for the purpose of truthfully advising the public," the proviso is explicitly limited to publicity "other than picketing." [9]

In the 1961 case of *Upholsterers Twin City Local 61 (Minneapolis House Furnishings Co.)*,[10] the Board continued to follow the same line of reasoning in applying section 8(b)(4)(ii)(B). Additionally, clearer distinctions were drawn between the requirements for violations of subsections (i) and (ii) of section 8(b)(4) (B). The facts involved were substantially identical to *Perfection Mattress*. The NLRB held that the union's picketing of the stores was not a violation of section 8(b)(4)(i)(B) because the picketing was aimed at consumers and not the employees of the secondary employers. It declared that "picketing at the secondary employer's premises alone is not per se 'inducement or encouragement' of employees within the meaning of clause (i)." [11] The determination of a violation, it was reasoned, should rest on the particular evidence involved. The facts in the current case indicated to the Board that there was no intent to induce a refusal to work by store employees and that, in fact, no such refusal occurred. Furthermore, there was no intended or actual interference with store pickups or deliveries.

On the basis of these same facts, however, the Board did find a violation of subsection (ii) of section 8(b)(4). The NLRB held that picketing appeals to consumers in front of retail stores was prohibited since they had the object of forcing the stores to cease or at least to curtail business with the non-union manufacturers. The Board's conclusion was based upon the simple proposition that all consumer picketing violated section 8(b)(4)(ii)(B).

The NLRB's early decisions dealing with consumer picketing not only effectuated the clear language of the statute, but also served to balance the conflicting interests of neutral secondary

---

[9] 129 N.L.R.B. at 1023.

[10] 132 N.L.R.B. 40 (1961), *rev'd*, 331 F.2d 561 (8th Cir. 1964). The court's reversal was based on the Supreme Court's decision in *Tree Fruits*.

[11] 132 N.L.R.B. at 41.

employers and of unions. In enunciating the policy of the 1959
amendments to the National Labor Relations Act, Congress recognized the need to prohibit secondary boycotts in order to protect
neutral employers. Certain exceptions have been formulated that
protect union interests in secondary boycott situations. Where the
secondary employer's premises constitute a part of a common or
roving situs [12] or where the secondary employer is an ally [13] of the
primary employer, a union is allowed to engage in activity at the
premises of the secondary employer that would otherwise be prohibited. Furthermore, where there is neither a common situs nor
an alliance, the secondary boycott section makes specific provisions
to safeguard union interests in publicizing its dispute with the
primary employer to the consuming public. Such publicity may
take place upon the premises of the neutral secondary employer
even when the secondary is not an ally of the primary employer
and when the premises are not part of a common situs. These
provisions are contained in the publicity proviso of section 8(b)
(4)(B).

Consumer Directed Publicity

The publicity proviso was interpreted and applied by the NLRB
in a manner that protected union handbilling in *Minneapolis House
Furnishings*.[14] The union had engaged in the distribution of leaf-
lets at the retail department stores while they also picketed these
sites. The union handbills contained an appeal to customers to
buy only locally and union made furniture and mattresses. The
Board ruled that even though the handbilling and the picketing
were conducted simultaneously, the two activities were distinct.
The picketing violated the Act, but the leaflet distribution was not
part of this picketing and was protected by the publicity proviso.

> While the proviso to Section 8(b)(4) does not define the per-
> missive publicity, the legislative history makes it abundantly clear
> that the Senate and House Conferees, who drafted the proviso,
> intended thereby to confer, subject to certain conditions, immunity
> on all forms of informational activity by unions, except picketing.[15]

[12] This is discussed in Chapter II *supra*.

[13] This is discussed in Chapter III *supra*.

[14] 132 N.L.R.B. 40 (1961), *rev'd*, 331 F.2d 561 (8th Cir. 1964).

[15] 132 NLRB at 46; 2 Legis. Hist. at 1432. In reporting on the amendments drafted by the conferees Senator Kennedy stated:

In thus ruling, the Board established that picketing in violation of the Act does not affect the legality of other informational activity that is conducted simultaneously. Although picketing is specifically excluded from the publicity proviso, other forms of publicity, subject to certain statutory conditions, may be covered within its ambit. Referring to these statutory conditions, the Board stated that

> In the instant case, the leaflets satisfied all three requirements specified in the proviso: (1) The leaflet was distributed "for the purpose of truthfully advising the public, including consumers and members of a labor organization," that the union was involved in a dispute. . . . It is true that the union was not involved in any *active* dispute with any of the nonarea manufacturers of boycotted products, but this is not necessary to bring the union conduct within the meaning of the term "primary dispute" as used in the proviso. It is sufficient that the interest of the union in protecting employment opportunities for its members and the interest of nonarea manufacturers in selling their products in the area became irreconcilable. . . . (2) The leaflet also satisfied the condition of the proviso that the publicity must not result in work stoppages by the employees of the secondary employer. None had occurred at the stores which were picketed; and (3) finally, as required by the proviso, the leaflet distribution here was "publicity other than picketing." [16]

In interpreting section 8(b)(4)(ii)(B) in a manner that prohibited picketing for consumer boycotts, the Board protected the interests of neutral secondary employers. At the same time, the interests of unions to convey information and to publicize their disputes with primary employers were protected by the publicity proviso subject to the flexible requirements set forth. The Board followed the clear language of the statute and the intent of the legislators. The wisdom of excluding picketing from the publicity proviso and of prohibiting consumer boycott picketing under section 8(b)(4)(ii)(B) is supported by the recognized fact that

---

. . . We were unable to persuade House conferees to permit picketing in front of that secondary shop, but we were able to persuade them to agree that the union shall be free to conduct informational activity short of picketing. In other words, the union can hand out handbills at the shop, can place advertisements in newspapers, can make announcements over the radio, and can carry on all publicity short of having ambulatory picketing in front of a secondary site.

[16] 132 NLRB at 46-7.

picketing has a so-called "signal effect" [17] which is harmful to the business of a secondary employer. The mere presence of pickets is more likely to discourage consumers completely from dealing with the neutral secondary employer. This same generalized effect is not to be found among other publicity techniques. Secondary consumer picketing was banned because it was much too effective and therefore the Board correctly viewed the operation of section 8(b)(4)(ii)(B) and the publicity proviso as an "accommodation between the right of neutral employers not to be coerced in the conduct of their business and the right of unions to engage in informational activity under the free-speech provision of the Constitution." [18]

Early NLRB decisions were completely in line with the 1959 amendments. Neutral secondary employers were protected from consumer boycotts that had been implemented by picketing. The publicity proviso effectively safeguarded the unions' right to publicize disputes by means other than picketing. The case law regarding union appeals to the consuming public at the premises of a secondary employer was settled. In 1964, the Supreme Court introduced a new doctrine that significantly changed this body of law.

THE TREE FRUITS DECISION

In 1964, the Supreme Court upset the delicate balance established by Congress and applied by the NLRB. The Court held that consumer picketing at the premises of a secondary employer is not prohibited where the union's appeal not to purchase is limited to the struck product and is not designed to stop all trade with the neutral secondary employer.

In *Fruit and Vegetable Packers Local 760 (Tree Fruits Labor Relations Committee)* [19] the NLRB relied on the well established position that secondary consumer picketing is banned under section 8(b)(4)(ii)(B) as an unfair labor practice. The union involved had had a primary dispute with a fruit packager and picketed the premises of Safeway supermarket stores in Seattle, Washington. The picket signs stated: "To the consumer: Non-Union Washington State apples are being sold in this store. Please do not purchase such apples. Thank you. Local 760, Yakima,

---

[17] *See* Comment, *Product Picketing—A New Loophole in Section 8(b)(4) (B) of the National Labor Relations Act?* 63 Mich. L. Rev. 682, 692 (1965).

[18] 132 N.L.R.B. at 47.

[19] 132 N.L.R.B. 1172 (1961), *enforcement denied*, 308 F.2d 311 (D.C. Cir. 1963), *aff'd*, 377 U.S. 58 (1964).

Washington." This legend was clearly directed at customers of Safeway and identified the product of the struck employer. Further, the pickets were conducted at customer entrances only during shopping hours. The picketing was peaceful and there was no interference with the Safeway employees or with the pickup and delivery of goods at the secondary premises. These facts were substantially similar to those in the *Perfection Mattress* and *Minneapolis House Furnishings* cases which the Board decided in 1960 and 1961. The Board concluded in *Tree Fruits* that the union had engaged in prohibited secondary activity, once again reasoning that by the literal language of the proviso to § 8(b) (4) (ii) (B) as well as by the legislative history of the section, consumer picketing in front of a secondary establishment is prohibited.

The Court of Appeals for the District of Columbia refused enforcement of the order on the grounds that there was no specific finding of the use of threats, coercion, or restraint to achieve the specified objectives.[20] The court reasoned that consumer picketing was not coercive per se and that in order to prohibit such activity there must be a showing of threats, coercion, or restraint.

The Supreme Court also upheld the picketing in *Tree Fruits*.[21] The Court reasoned that not every instance of consumer picketing at a secondary premises is prohibited. It did not find the legislative history to be sufficiently convincing that the intent of Congress was to ban all peaceful secondary consumer picketing. The majority felt that "it does not follow from the fact that some coercive conduct was protected by the proviso, that the exception 'other than picketing' indicates that Congress had determined that all consumer picketing was coercive."[22]

Despite the Court's holding, the legislative history seems quite clear in its prohibition of secondary consumer picketing. Activity that is not protected by the proviso is subject to section 8(b) (4) (ii) (B). Prior NLRB decisions were reasonable in light of the statutory language, the legislative history, and the equitable protection of the interests of concerned parties. By allowing the consumer boycott picketing of Safeway, the Court made law that finds much less support in the statute and in the legislative history than do the prior decisions reached by the NLRB.

---

[20] 308 F.2d 311.

[21] 377 U.S. 58 (1964).

[22] *Id.* at 69.

The Supreme Court's *Tree Fruits* decision created a new exception which distinguishes between a total and a partial consumer boycott. The substance of the Court's holding was that total consumer boycott picketing was banned by the Act but that partial consumer boycott picketing is to be allowed:

> When consumer picketing is employed only to persuade customers not to buy the struck product, the union's appeal is closely confined to the primary dispute. The site of the appeal is expanded to include the premises of the secondary employer, but if the appeal succeeds, the secondary employer's purchases from the struck firm are decreased only because the public had diminished its purchases of the struck product. On the other hand, when consumer picketing is employed to persuade customers not to trade at all with the secondary employer, the latter stops buying the struck product, not because of a falling demand, but in response to pressure designed to inflict injury on his business generally. In such a case, the union does more than merely follow the struck product, it creates a separate dispute with the secondary employer.[23]

There is no support for this distinction either in the language of section 8(b)(4)(B) or in the legislative history of the amendments. The Court supported its decision by reasoning that the "isolated evil" which Congress intended to correct was coercion of the secondary employer. The majority felt that the necessary element of coercion was absent in the case of consumer picketing used only to persuade customers not to buy the struck product of the primary employer. It stated that even when such pickets were successful and the secondary employer decreased his order of the struck product, the cause was not union coercion but a decline in public demand for the product.

The Court's distinction between a total and a partial consumer boycott rests upon underlying and minor differences in the degree of coercion. The decision defines total consumer picketing, aimed at convincing consumers to cease all trade with the secondary employer, as being within the statutory requirements of coercion. Partial consumer picketing, aimed at convincing consumers to cease trading with the secondary employer only as to the struck product, is interpreted as being permissible and not within the statutory requirements of coercion. The Court held that based on this distinction the union's appeal in a partial boycott is closely confined to the primary dispute, even though the site of the appeal is expanded. This distinction is somewhat unrealistic.

---

[23] *Id.* at 72.

In both cases the effects of union consumer picketing upon the secondary employer far surpass the effects of a normal and successful stirke. In the case of a successful strike, the secondary employer is prevented from trading in the struck product because of a dwindling supply. A successful strike affects the supply of and not the demand for a product. Even in those instances where a strike is attributed with decreasing demand, the relationship is quite indirect and usually insignificant. On the other hand, consumer picketing, whether it be of a total or a partial nature, directly influences the sale of goods by the secondary employer by decreasing the demand for a product or products. All consumer picketing influences demand and thus has a direct effect upon the secondary employer's decision to continue dealing with the primary employer. Partial boycotts, like total boycotts, involve added elements of restraint and coercion that do not arise from and are not confined to the primary dispute.

In a concurring opinion, Mr. Justice Black stated that the wording of the section and the legislative history clearly do not support the majority's decision. Reasoning, however, that the section violates the Constitution, he commented:

> Because of the language of § 8(b) (4) (ii) (B) of the National Labor Relations Act and the legislative history set out in the opinions of the Court and of my Brother Harlan, I feel impelled to hold that Congress, in passing this section of the Act, intended to forbid the striking employees of one business to picket the premises of a neutral business where the purpose of the picketing is to persuade customers of the neutral business not to buy goods supplied by the struck employer. Construed in this way, as I agree with Brother Harlan that it must be, I believe, contrary to his view, that the section abridges freedom of speech and press in violation of the First Amendment.[24]

This article is not directly concerned with the constitutional issues of free speech that arose. We do feel, however, that the section's prohibition of secondary consumer picketing would likely receive judicial sanction, despite Mr. Justice Black's view, on the basis of the legislative policy of protecting neutral employers.[25]

Portions of Justice Black's opinion agreed with the dissent of Mr. Justice Harlan. Harlan found clear evidence in the legislative history that section 8(b) (4) (B) was intended to prohibit consumer picketing in connection with secondary boycotts. Further-

---

[24] *Id.* at 76.

[25] *See* Teamsters Local 695 v. Vogt, Inc. 354 U.S. 284 (1957).

more, the facts presented in *Tree Fruits* were obviously encompassed by the statutory language.

> The Union's activities are plainly within the letter of subdivision
> (4)(ii)(B) of §8(b), and indeed the Court's opinion virtually
> concedes that much. Certainly, Safeway is a "person" as defined in
> those subdivisions; indubitably "an object" of the Union's conduct
> was the "forcing or requiring" of Safeway, through the picketing
> of its customers, "to cease . . . selling, handling . . . or otherwise
> dealing in" Washington apples, "the products of" another "producer;" and consumer picketing is expressly excluded from the
> ameliorative provisions of the proviso.[26]

The dissenting opinion makes a very convincing case as to the erroneous nature of the majority's decision. The facts presented in *Tree Fruits* squarely fit the provisions of the section that forbid secondary boycotts and appear to be precisely the situation which the framers of the Landrum-Griffin Amendments desired to proscribe.

The purpose of the 1959 amendments was to protect neutral employers from secondary pressure, including consumer picketing. The publicity proviso was to have the intended effect of preserving the interests and rights of unions to publicize their labor disputes. The statutory scheme, therefore, was to protect neutral employers from coercive pressure while allowing unions to use means other than picketing to publicize the sale of struck products. This balanced statutory scheme was destroyed under the *Tree Fruits* doctrine. Union power was greatly increased and neutral employers were now exposed to secondary pressures.

The effect of the *Tree Fruits* decision was to weaken that element of the statute that was intended to protect neutrals, while leaving unaffected the union's protection under the publicity proviso. The statutory balance mandated by Congress was further upset by another Supreme Court case, decided practically in conjunction with *Tree Fruits*, which extended union power by redefining and broadening the scope of the publicity proviso.

PUBLICITY PROVISO

The publicity proviso is an important part of the statutory scheme of maintaining union rights while protecting secondary employers. A union may publicize to consumers that a product, produced by an employer with whom it has a dispute, is being dis-

---

[26] 377 U.S. 58, 82.

tributed by another employer. According to the terms of the statute, the union may use any means of publicity other than picketing. Because the wording of the proviso and the legislative hsitory are not very specific, the Board and the courts have had great latitude in interpreting the scope of the provisions.

NLRB and Circuit Court Positions

It will be recalled that in *Minneapolis House Furnishings*, examined above, the NLRB held that the simultaneous occurrence of leaflet distribution and picketing activity does not mean that the activities are to be joined together for purposes of determining legality.[27] Therefore, despite the illegal picketing, the handbilling was protected as publicity in that use. The NLRB found that the legislative history of the proviso called for a broad application of its protection to all publicity other than picketing. It held that the proviso not only allowed handbills, but also allowed unfair lists, newspaper advertisements, and radio broadcasts as legitimate means of publicity.

Milk Drivers and Dairy Employees Local 537 (Lohman Sales Co.)[28] provided the NLRB with a slightly varied fact situation which required thorough examination of the proviso. The primary employer was a wholesale distributor of cigarettes, cigars, other tobacco products, and candy. The union, on strike against the primary employer, distributed handbills at retail drugstores urging customers not to buy Lohman products. The Board decided that even though the leaflet distribution was accompanied by coercive oral appeals, which by themselves violated § 8(b)(4)(i)(B), the activity was publicity and therefore entitled to protection.

In reaching this determination, the Board faced the difficult issue of whether Lohman produced a product, as required by the proviso, or whether it merely handled a product produced by others. The proviso specifically states that the publicity must be "for the purpose of truthfully advising the public . . . that a product or products are produced by an employer with whom the labor organization has a primary dispute." [29] The Board held that Lohman, a distributor of tobacco goods and candy manufactured by others, was a producer of these goods within the meaning of the proviso. A broad

---

[27] 132 N.L.R.B. 40 (1961), *rev'd*, 331 F.2d 561 (8th Cir. 1964).

[28] 132 N.L.R.B. 901 (1961).

[29] Labor-Management Reporting and Disclosure Act of 1959, § 704, 29 U.S.C. § 158(b)(4)(B).

interpretation of the publicity provisions serves to extend union power. Such an extension would seem desirable only if it is counterbalanced by the prohibitions in section 8(b)(4)(ii)(B).

The NLRB further defined the term "producer" in *American Television and Radio Artists (Great Western Broadcasting Corp.)*,[30] where it held that a television station was a "producer" for purposes of the publicity proviso. Consequently, handbilling by the station's employees at the premises of secondary employers who advertised on the station was protected activity under *Lohman*.

The Circuit Court of Appeals for the Ninth Circuit disagreed with this result.[31] It stated that even though the legislative history was inconclusive as to the intended meaning of "producer," the wording of the proviso itself was sufficiently clear to exclude television advertising. The court commented that

> . . . the context in which the term "product" appears in the proviso precludes the view that the television service rendered by KYTV, considered alone, is a "product" within the meaning of the proviso. One reason for this conclusion is the fact that in two other places in section 8(b)(4), the term services is used in contradistinction to tangible articles. It is likely that Congress would have followed the same format if it had intended the publicity proviso to apply with regard to a primary employer who renders services instead of manufactures tangible articles.[32]

The court went on to reason that the statute required that the "products" be capable of being distributed by another employer and that television advertising service did not meet this test. In reaching such a conclusion, the court specifically overruled the NLRB's finding that for the purposes of the proviso the distributed product was the advertised item rather than the advertising service and that therefore the "product" was capable of distribution. This conflict was to be resolved by the Supreme Court in *Servette*.

The Supreme Court Reaction

The dispute between the NLRB and the Ninth Circuit Court of Appeals created a conflict which could only be settled by the

---

[30] 134 N.L.R.B. 1617 (1961), *rev'd*, 310 F.2d 591 (9th Cir. 1962).

[31] 310 F.2d 591.

[32] *Id.* at 595-6.

Supreme Court. *NLRB v. Servette*,[33] the vehicle used by the Court, involved a primary employer engaged in wholesale food distribution whose employees distributed handbills at supermarket chain stores that were customers of the primary employer. The NLRB, following its reasoning in *Lohman* and *Great Western*, held that a wholesale food distributor was a producer within the meaning of the publicity proviso and thus the handbilling activity was protected. The Court of Appeals for the Ninth Circuit refused to enforce the NLRB order. Relying on its earlier decisions, the court held that the publicity proviso was inapplicable since the primary employer was a distributor and not a producer.

On certiorari, the Supreme Court adopted the broad construction given to the proviso by the NLRB. After reviewing the proviso's legislative history and broad statutory interpretations, the Court concluded:

> There is nothing in the legislative history which suggests that the protection of the proviso was intended to be any narrower in coverage than the prohibition to which it is an exception, and we see no basis for attributing such an incongruous purpose to Congress.[34]

Following the Supreme Court's decision in *Servette*, *Great Western Broadcasting*[35] came up on remand before the NLRB. The Board, and subsequently the Ninth Circuit Court, relied upon *Servette* to again hold that services were "products" within the publicity proviso. Attempting to summarize the scope of the proviso after *Servette*, the Board members commented:

> While *Servette* and *Lohman* both involved wholesalers of a physical product, we are of the opinion that the Supreme Court's decision in *Servette* sustains our holding enunciated in *Lohman*, that "producer" as used in the proviso, encompasses anyone who enhances the economic value of the product ultimately sold or consumed; i.e. for the purposes of the proviso, no distinction is drawn between processors, distributors, and those supplying services. Since the Court has stated that the protection of the proviso is not "any narrower in coverage than the prohibition to which it is an exception," and since the prohibition of Section 8(b)(4)(B) covers the

---

[33] 377 U.S. 46 (1964), *rev'g*, 310 F.2d 659 (9th Cir. 1963), *enforcing* 133 N.L.R.B. 1501 (1961).

[34] 377 U.S. at 55.

[35] American Television and Radio Artists Local 55 (Great Western Broadcasting Corp.), 150 N.L.R.B. 467 (1964), *aff'd*, 356 F.2d 434 (9th Cir. 1966).

performance of services as well as processing or distribution of physical products, it follows that the proviso likewise applies to the performance of services.[36]

The significance of these decisions is their direct relationship to and affect upon consumer boycotts. In the *Servette* case, the Supreme Court's ruling established a policy that greatly expanded the rights of unions to engage in activity to publicize its labor dispute with an employer. The union was allowed to publicize its dispute and to appeal to consumers through almost any means except picketing. After the *Tree Fruits* decision, picketing for such purposes also became lawful. As a result of *Servette* these activities may be undertaken not only in the case of a primary employer who is a manufacturer, but also where the primary employer is a distributor, processor, or a supplier of services. The *Servette* decision does not violate either the legislative history or the wording of the Act. While its effect is to augment union power, the *Servette* decision by itself does not significantly decrease the protection afforded neutral employers under the Act. However, the rights of neutrals are dangerously affected by *Servette* when read in conjunction with *Tree Fruits*. The latter case greatly weakens the protection of neutral employers while the former expands the power of unions to carry a dispute to the premises of the secondary employer.

The *Tree Fruits* doctrine can only be regarded as having been created by the judiciary. Its application to other cases of consumer picketing is not automatic. Regardless of the wisdom of the rule, the *Tree Fruits* doctrine has become established law. Nevertheless, the very real question remains whether it should be applied as a general rule or as a judicially created exception to the mandates contained in section 8(b)(4)(ii)(B). Reliance upon the *Tree Fruits* doctrine as a rule of general application further endangers neutral employers. Realizing the difficulty of overruling such a decision, a more desirable policy would be to confine the doctrine to the facts from which it arose and to regard it as a limited exception to the general statutory principles.

Unfortunately, a review of subsequent decisions reveals that the *Tree Fruits* doctrine, which began as an exception, has since become the general rule. The consequences of this somewhat hidden evolution are indeed deserving of examination.

---

[36] 150 N.L.R.B. at 472.

THE TREE FRUITS DOCTRINE EXTENDED

The *Tree Fruits* decision represents a major turning point in secondary boycott law. Picketing for the purpose of imposing a partial, rather than total, consumer boycott upon a neutral employer was no longer prohibited. The scope of this judicially created doctrine is closely tied to the fact situation from which it arose. In *Tree Fruits* the struck product, apples, was easily identified and substantially unchanged in the hands of the retailer. Further, the struck product was only one of several products carried by the retail store. Once a variation of these facts arises, difficult questions involving the application of the doctrine are presented. Mr. Justice Harlan revealed an acute awareness of this problem when he commented in his dissent in *Tree Fruits,* "The distinction drawn by the majority becomes even more tenuous if a picketed retailer depends largely or entirely on the sales of the struck product." [37]

In such situations, the boycott that is aimed only at the struck product and thus only partially at the business of the secondary employer, becomes indistinguishable from the total boycott which is geared to persuade consumers to cease all trade with the secondary employer. Indeed, serious problems arise once even simple factual variations are introduced. Justice Harlan's comments were soon to be proven prophetic. The Board and courts have been faced with such variations of consumer picketing activity.

Extent of Appeal

One of the most common problems that arises under the *Tree Fruits* doctrine is whether the picketing appeal is intended to induce consumers to stop dealing in the struck product or to induce a cessation of all trade with the secondary employer. *Furniture Workers Local 140 (U.S. Mattress Corp.)* [38] involved a union dispute with a nonunion manufacturer of bedding. In furtherance of this dispute, the union conducted consumer picketing at retail stores carrying the bedding produced by the primary employer. The signs carried at the neutral furniture stores urged the consuming public to refrain from buying nonunion label furniture but did not specify the nonunion manufacturer or its product. The NLRB held that under these circumstances the picketing was not protected

---

[37] 377 U.S. 58, 83.

[38] 164 N.L.R.B. 271 (1967), *enforced,* 390 F.2d 495 (2d Cir. 1968).

by the *Tree Fruits* doctrine. The picketing appeal was overly broad and the object of the picketing was to force the cessation of business between the neutral secondary employers and U.S. Mattress.

> Unlike the union in *Tree Fruits*, Respondent did not by the legend on its picket sign, or otherwise, define the limits of its dispute by clearly identifying the primary employer or its products so as to make readily apparent to the consuming public precisely against whom its boycott appeal was directed.[39]

The *U.S. Mattress* case calls for the application of the *Tree Fruits* line of reasoning. Because the product of the primary employer was readily identifiable and substantially unchanged and was only one of several other items sold by the secondary employer, the *Tree Fruits* rationale was properly applied. Since the scope of the picketing appeals was overly broad, the picketing here imposed a total boycott which is prohibited under the exception created by the Supreme Court. Where the facts presented by the case vary and the product is not identifiable or is substantially changed in the hands of the secondary, it becomes extremely difficult and confusing to apply the reasoning of the *Tree Fruits* exception rather than the general rule of the statute that prohibits such activity.

Integrated Products

One of the problems faced by the NLRB has involved situations where the product of the primary employer becomes an integral part of the product offered for sale by the secondary employer. In *Millmen and Cabinet Makers Local 550 (Steiner Lumber Co.)*,[40] the primary employer, Steiner, sold lumber to the secondary employer, Besco, who built and sold houses. As part of its dispute with Steiner the union conducted picketing at the construction project of the secondary employer appealing to consumers not to buy the lumber used in building the houses. The union alleged that this activity was protected by the *Tree Fruits* doctrine. Disagreeing, the Trial Examiner reasoned that the picketing here was to convince the consumer to cease all business with the secondary employer. Even if the picketing was consumer oriented, the object was a total boycott "since a home buyer could scarcely buy a home . . . without purchasing the lumber in the home." [41] The

---

[39] 164 N.L.R.B. at 273.

[40] 153 N.L.R.B. 1285 (1965), *enforced*, 367 F.2d 953 (9th Cir. 1966).

[41] 153 N.L.R.B. at 1290.

Tree Fruits doctrine, the examiner concluded, was inapplicable in such cases and thus the consumer picketing was violative of the statutory mandate.

Although affirming the decision of the Trial Examiner, the NLRB circumvented the problem of applying *Tree Fruits* by relying upon section 8(b)(4)(ii)(B). It held that the consumer picketing was a sham and that the real objective was to induce secondary employees to refuse to work. By adopting this reasoning the Board was able to avoid the difficulties of trying to reconcile *Tree Fruits* with cases in which the struck product is so highly integrated with the final product that they become inseparable.

In *Twin City Carpenters District Council (Red Wing Wood Products, Inc.)*[42] the NLRB was presented with a similar problem. Here the primary employer made kitchen cabinets which were sold to Pempton for installation in the new houses. The union picketed at the new houses asking that the consumer refrain from buying the cabinets. Finding a violation of section 8(b)(4)(ii)(B), the Board ruled that since the legend on the picket signs failed to identify the primary employer, the picketing was too broad and thus was intended to force the neutral contractor to cease doing business with Red Wing.

The NLRB has avoided making a clear determination as to the role of the *Tree Fruits* doctrine in cases where the product of the primary employer becomes an integral part of the product of the neutral secondary employer. Ignoring the significance of the difference in facts between these cases and those in *Tree Fruits*, the NLRB has chosen rather to rely on technical requirements. The results reached by the NLRB in cases involving integrated products have been correct. However, in reaching these results the NLRB approach has been to rely on *Tree Fruits* as the determining factor. Where the product is an integrated part of a product in the hands of a secondary employer, *Tree Fruits* has no legitimate application. The NLRB's policy leaves much room for a widening of the *Tree Fruits* exception and for greater avoidance of the statutory prohibitions in future cases.

Where the struck product is highly integrated with the neutral employer's product, the *Tree Fruits* exception should be inapplicable and the standards of 8(b)(4)(ii)(B) applied. The product of the primary employer is so much a part of the final product that it cannot be separated. A boycott of the struck product becomes a total boycott of the entire business of the secondary employer, a

---

[42] 167 N.L.R.B. 1017 (1967), *enforced*, 422 F.2d 309 (8th Cir. 1970).

situation prohibited by law. The *Tree Fruits* exception should not be extended to cases of this type since the fundamental distinction upon which it is based does not exist in such situations. The consequences of such consumer picketing exceed even those forseen by Justice Harlan in his *Tree Fruits* dissent. Consumer picketing of an integrated struck product affects many more parties than in the situation envisioned by Harlan. The struck product cannot be picketed without affecting the products of many other parties whose work is also a part of the finished goods. In order to protect these many neutrals, national labor policy demands that the *Tree Fruits* doctrine be abandoned and that the statute be applied as intended.

Loss of Product Identity

Taxi Drivers Local 237 (American Bread Co.)[43] presented the Board with a unique factual variation of *Tree Fruits*. The product of the primary employer, bread, was held to lose its identity when served to restaurant customers. The picketing of restaurants serving the struck product was prohibited because its effect was to force the secondary employer to cease doing business with the bread bakers. The decision by the NLRB was based on the *Tree Fruits* doctrine. Since the customer could not identify the struck product, the picketing took on an objective of imposing a total boycott. Although the result reached here was proper, once again the NLRB decision failed to clarify the role of *Tree Fruits* in such situations. The Board found that the picketing here was not protected by *Tree Fruits* because the appeal went beyond the struck product. The NLRB has not held, as it should, that *Tree Fruits* cannot be applied where the struck product cannot be readily identified by the consuming public. Once the struck product loses its identity there can no longer be a limited, partial boycott of only the struck product. The Board has failed to clarify this point.

Once the identity of the struck product is lost, the relationship of that product to the consuming public becomes extremely indirect. Little importance attaches to the question of whether the union activity was consumer oriented. The significant inquiry under section 8(b)(4)(ii)(B) is simply whether the activity and its objective impose penalties upon neutral secondary parties.

---

[43] 170 N.L.R.B. No. 19, 67 L.R.R.M. 1427 (1968), *enforced in part*, 411 F.2d 147 (6th Cir. 1969).

Struck Service Industry

The confusion resulting from the application of the *Tree Fruits* doctrine to cases involving factual variations became most apparent in a case wherein the struck product of the primary employer was an intangible service—advertising. The *Honolulu Typographical Union No. 37 (Hawaii Press Newspapers)*[44] involved a union dispute with a newspaper publisher. The union conducted consumer picketing at the entrance of a shopping center housing fifty to sixty stores, of which six were advertisers in the primary employer's newspaper. The picket signs bore the names of the advertising employers and urged the public not to buy goods advertised in the newspaper involved. Five of the employers were restaurants which had advertised their entire menus. The sixth employer was a jewelry store which advertised selected goods. In no case had the union listed the goods advertised in the paper. In deciding that the picketing was in violation of the Act, both the Board and the Court of Appeals for the District of Columbia relied on the distinction between total and partial boycotts.

> A loss of patronage resulting from the picketing appeal could have no direct impact upon the restaurants' need for further advertising; indeed a reduction of patronage under normal circumstances might well lead to a desire and need for more advertising. Thus the picketing of the restaurants in this case constituted more than a mere following of a struck product in a *Tree Fruits* sense; its obvious aim was to cause a cessation of the secondary employer's dealings with the primary employer, not as a natural consequence of a falling consumer demand, but by force of the injury that would otherwise be inflicted on their businesses generally.[45]

The Board and court went to great lengths in order to frame an argument in terms of *Tree Fruits* and yet to achieve the desired result of prohibiting picketing of integrated and unidentifiable products. In situations of this type, there is no product sufficient for the *Tree Fruits* purposes of imposing only a partial boycott that is confined to the product of the primary employer.

The NLRB and court agreed that the picketing of the jewelry store imposed a total boycott. Since the advertised products were not identified, the picketing was not closely confined to the primary

---

[44] 167 N.L.R.B. 1030 (1967), *enforced*, 401 F.2d 952 (D.C. Cir. 1968).

[45] 167 N.L.R.B. at 1032.

dispute.[46] The application of the *Tree Fruits* doctrine to this type
of case creates a potential situation which would allow the union
to exert pressure on the secondary employer. If the advertisements
did not encompass the entire business of the neutral employer and
if the picket signs identified the advertised products, the clear
implication is that this type of secondary pressure would have been
allowed. Such an interpretation would have imposed a secondary
boycott not only upon the advertising employer, but also upon the
producers of the advertised goods. *Tree Fruits* is misapplied in
such situations. The application of these tests to situations wherein
the struck product is an inseparable part of the final product is
clearly erroneous.

CONCLUDING REMARKS

Before 1964, the NLRB and the courts consistently held that
section 8(b)(4)(ii)(B) prohibited unions from picketing at the
premises of neutral secondary employers in order to enhance their
bargaining power. The decisions of both the Board and the courts
maintained an equitable balance between union and neutral employer interests in order to preserve stable labor relations.

The delicate balance of these conflicting interests was seriously
disturbed by the Supreme Court in 1964. *Tree Fruits* was a highly
controversial decision that seemed to contravene both the terms of
the statute and the intent of the legislature in enacting the 1959
Landrum-Griffin amendments. Even on the basis of the particular
fact situation presented in *Tree Fruits* there is little support for the
Supreme Court's decision. Nevertheless, the doctrine of that case
is now accepted law.

Serious difficulties have arisen over the scope and application of
the doctrine. Any extension of its application to uses involving
factual variations should be carefully avoided. In such cases,
secondary pressure can be exerted on an even greater scale upon
the neutral employer and his suppliers. Unions have the statutory
right to truthfully publicize the existence of a dispute to the consuming public through means other than picketing at the premises
of the secondary employer. In addition, it has been held that such
publicity may appeal to consumers to stop all trade with secondary

---

[46] *See also* Atlanta Typographical Union No. 48 (Times-Journal, Inc.),
180 N.L.R.B. No. 164, 73 LRRM 1241 (1970); Los Angeles Typographical
Union No. 174 (White Front Stores), 181 N.L.R.B. No. 61, 73 LRRM 1390
(1970).

employers, even though such broad appeals may not be made by picketing.

> That the Court did not view the proviso, or its standards, as con-
> trolling consumer picketing is underscored by the careful distinc-
> tion the Court drew between the proviso—authorized publicity,
> which the Court found allowed a union to persuade the customers
> of a secondary employer to stop all trade with him, and per-
> missable consumer picketing, which the Court made clear did not
> extend to such a broadside appeal.[47]

Under such an interpretation of the publicity proviso, the union's right to publicize its labor disputes and to urge certain public co-operation remain protected. It is indeed unfortunate that an equal degree of protection for the neutral secondary employer from the effects of consumer picketing has not been maintained.

The *Tree Fruits* rule must be construed as an exception to the general rule that prohibits consumer picketing. It must be applied on a narrow basis and confined to factual cases similar to the one from which it arose. The NLRB and courts have failed to com-prehend the importance of limiting the *Tree Fruits* doctrine. In-stead, recent Board and court decisions have relied on the Supreme Court's *Tree Fruits* decision as establishing a rule of general applicability.

The current view seems to be that under *Tree Fruits* all con-sumer picketing is protected. Picketing geared to impose a total boycott of the secondary employer is not consumer picketing be-cause it is coercive and is not to be protected. Such a view makes the administration of this area of labor law unnecessarily confus-ing. It is much clearer and more correct to view section 8(b)(4) (ii)(B) as prohibiting all consumer picketing and to view *Tree Fruits* as a judicially created exception applicable only to those cases presenting similar fact patterns. The recent decisions have produced results that greatly strain the *Tree Fruits* exception and fail to rely on the general statutory rule prohibiting consumer picketing. The extension of the *Tree Fruits* rationale to cases involving factual variations totally ignores the interests of neutral secondary employers and serves only to introduce even greater confusion to this complex area of labor relations.

---

[47] 167 N.L.R.B. 1030, 1031.

CHAPTER V

Hot-Cargo Agreements

Unlike the secondary boycott situations dealt with in other sections of this study, the hot-cargo agreement involves a provision in a collective bargaining contract. Under the terms of such contract clauses, the union and the employer agree that employees of the contracting employer may refuse to use or to handle the products of other, or secondary, employers in certain circumstances. Prior to the passage of the 1959 Landrum-Griffin Amendments, these circumstances most commonly involved products that were nonunion or "unfair" or struck goods. After 1959, hot-cargo clauses sought to protect employee refusals to cross or work behind picket lines or to handle struck or nonunion goods, and also sought to govern subcontracting and work allocation.

Like other secondary boycott situations, these hot-cargo clauses often serve to enmesh neutral employers in labor disputes that are not their own. And like all secondary boycotts, they involve important but conflicting interests of unions and of neutral secondary employers and consumers. Where labor disputes extend beyond the primary parties, it becomes the task of the NLRB and of the courts to resolve the problem in a manner that balances the conflicting interests of unions to exert pressure on the primary employer and of secondary employers to remain neutral. This chapter seeks to examine and to assess the role of the Board and of the courts in accomplishing this task with regard to hot-cargo clauses.

BEFORE LANDRUM-GRIFFIN:
FROM CONWAY'S EXPRESS TO SAND DOOR

Prior to the passage of the 1959 amendments, hot-cargo clauses were governed by section 8(b)(4)(A) of the National Labor Relations Act as amended by the Taft-Hartley Act of 1947. That section stated:

> 8(b) It shall be an unfair labor practice for a labor organization or its agents—
>
> . . .

(4) to engage in, or to induce or encourage the employees of any employer to engage in, a strike or a concerted refusal in the course of their employment to use, manufacture, process, transport, or otherwise handle or work on any goods, articles, materials, or commodities or to perform any services, where an object thereof is:

> (A) forcing or requiring . . . any employer or other person to cease using, selling, handling, transporting, or otherwise dealing in the products of any other producer, processor, or manufacturer, or to cease to do business with any other person; . . .[1]

The above statutory provision did not deal specifically with contract clauses which allowed employees to refuse to handle unfair, nonunion, or struck goods. The Board and courts have had a great deal of difficulty in applying the terms of the statute to situations in which contract clauses allowing such refusals have been enforced against secondary parties.

Conway's Express: Original NLRB View

Teamsters Local 294 (Conway's Express)[2] was the first hot-cargo case to come before the Board after the passage of section 8(b)(4)(A). This case involved an area agreement between several employers and the union. The terms of the contract clauses reserved to the union the right to refuse to handle goods or freight of any employer involved in a labor dispute. The union engaged in a strike against Conway for an alleged violation of Conway's contractual obligation to hire only union drivers. In furtherance of this strike, the union called upon the employees of the secondary employers to refuse to handle Conway's freight in accordance with the union's contract with their employers.

Under these circumstances, the NLRB and the Second Circuit Court of Appeals found that section 8(b)(4)(A) had not been violated. The Board held that section 8(b)(4)(A) was intended to prohibit only secondary boycotts and not strikes that are in furtherance of a legitimate primary dispute. Further, the Board stated that the conduct here involved was not a strike or a refusal since the secondary employers consented in advance to boycott Conway and the union's actions merely caused the employees to exercise their contractual rights.

---

[1] Labor Management Relations Act (Taft-Hartley Act), § 8(b)(4)(A), 61 Stat. 141 (1947), *as amended*, 29 U.S.C. § 158(b)(4)(A) (1964).

[2] 87 N.L.R.B. 972 (1949), *aff'd*, Rabouin v. NLRB, 195 F.2d 906 (2d Cir. 1952).

Section 8(b)(4)(A) of the Act prohibits *labor organizations* from "forcing or requiring" the participation of neutral employers in secondary boycotts by the use of certain forms of employee pressure, namely, strikes or work stoppages, (either actually engaged in, or "induced" or "encouraged" by the union). This section does not proscribe other means by which unions may induce employers to aid them in effectuating secondary boycotts; much less does it prohibit *employers* from refusing to deal with other persons, whether because they desire to aid a labor organization in the protection of its working standards, or for other reasons. An employer remains free, under that section of the amended Act, as always, to deal with whatever firms, union or nonunion, he chooses. And by the same token, there is nothing in the express provisions or underlying policy of Section 8(b)(4)(A) which prohibits an employer and a union from voluntarily including "hot cargo" or "struck work" provisions in their collective bargaining contracts, or from honoring these provisions.[3]

The reasoning of the Board amounted to a very technical application of the letter of the law in a manner that completely ignored and undermined the spirit and underlying policy of section 8(b)(4)(A). The effect of the *Conway* decision was to allow unions to contract for secondary boycotts that would be illegal had the contract provision been absent. Board Member Reynolds felt that the majority opinion ignored the realities of the situation.

The Act . . . unequivocally proscribes secondary activity on the part of unions. To the extent that these contract provisions authorize such activity, they are repugnant to the basic public policies of the Act. As the Board in the public interest is charged with the duty of preventing unfair labor practices, contracts which are repugnant to the Act and which conflict with this duty of the Board must obviously yield. Unions or employers cannot nullify the provisions of the Act which circumscribe their activities by inducing each other, or employers, to agree by contract in advance to waive their respective rights under the Act.[4]

The *Conway's Express* decision and other similar cases, such as *Pittsburgh Plate Glass*,[5] did indeed ignore the policy underlying section 8(b)(4)(A). Because there was no "inducement" or "en-

---

[3] 87 N.L.R.B. at 982-3.

[4] *Id.* at 995.

[5] *See* Teamsters Local 135 (Pittsburgh Plate Glass), 105 N.L.R.B. 740 (1953) in which the Board held that the refusal of employees of various trucking firms to handle freight of a struck union employer was permissible under an unfair goods provision of a contract between the union and the truckers.

Milk Drivers Local 338 (Crowley's Milk Co.)[11] presented similar issues to the Foard and the Second Circuit Court of Appeals. The NLRB here relied on the rules set forth originally in *McAllister* and found that the union had violated the Act. The court, however, found that since the unions had only encouraged the employees to exercise their contractual right to which the secondary employers had agreed there was no coercion of secondary employers and therefore no violation of the Act.

The legal status of the hot-cargo agreement was quite unclear as a result of the divergent views of the NLRB and some of the circuit courts. Often when such a clear conflict exists between the Board and the courts, it falls upon the Supreme Court to resolve the matter.

Sand Door: Judicial Compromise

The case that was to be the vehicle for Supreme Court action was *Carpenters Local 1976 (Sand Door and Plywood Co.).*[12] This case involved a hot-cargo contract clause that provided that employees of construction contractor Havstad and Jensen would not be required to handle nonunion goods. The product involved was nonunion doors manufactured by Paine Lumber Company and supplied to Havstad and Jensen by Sand Door. As the result of union appeals to the employees of the secondary employers, the doors were not installed. The NLRB holding in this case followed *McAllister* to the extent that the hot-cargo clause was not a defense to section 8(b)(4)(A). The finding of a violation, however, was based upon distinctions that had not previously been relied on by the Board. A distinction was drawn between union appeals to contracting secondary employers and appeals to their employees for enforcement of a hot-cargo provision. A violation arises, in this view, only in the latter case. The Ninth Circuit Court of Appeals followed the same rationale and reached the same result.

The Supreme Court's holding established that the mere execution of a hot-cargo agreement was not prima-facie evidence of prohibited inducement of employees. The Court also held, however, that a hot-cargo provision cannot be a defense to a charge of an unfair labor practice under section 8(b)(4)(A) when, in the

---

[11] 116 N.L.R.B. 1408 (1956), *rev'd,* 245 F.2d 817 (2d Cir. 1957), *rev'd,* 357 U.S. 345 (1958). The Supreme Court decision followed *Sand Door.*

[12] 113 N.L.R.B. 1210 (1955), *aff'd,* 241 F.2d 147 (9th Cir. 1957), *rev'd in part,* 357 U.S. 93 (1958).

absence of such a provision, the union conduct would unquestionably be a violation. In addition, the Court carried forth the distinction between union appeals to employees and union appeals
to employers for enforcement of a hot-cargo clause. Unions may
not make appeals directly to the employees of the contracting
employer to refuse to handle goods.

Following the decision in *Sand Door,* the law governing hot-
cargo clauses took the form of a compromise between the conflicting positions of prior Board and court decisions.

> The status of the hot cargo agreement after the *Sand Door* decision
> seemed to have been defined. A secondary employer could still
> voluntarily engage in a boycott for his own business purposes
> and a union could still approach an employer and attempt to per-
> suade him to engage in a boycott, but the union was prohibited
> from inducing the employees to refuse to handle the goods. *Sand
> Door* thus rejected the idea that the congressional purpose of
> enacting § 8(b)(4)(A) was to give the primary employer or the
> general public full protection against a secondary boycott.[13]

The effect of *Sand Door* was to overrule *Conway,* but only partially since hot-cargo clauses were not declared contrary to public
policy. Because there is nothing in the legislative history of the
Act which established that Congress had specifically intended to
govern hot-cargo clauses of section 8(b)(4)(A), the Court established a judicial compromise that permitted hot-cargo contracts to
stand except for those situations which would give rise to a
secondary boycott, irrespective of the existence of these contractual
provisions. The Court stated that

> . . . it is the business of Congress to declare policy and not this
> Court's. The judicial function is confined to applying what Con-
> gress has enacted after ascertaining what it is that Congress
> has enacted.[14]

The Court's decision was based upon the language of section
8(b)(4)(A) which prohibited the inducement or encouragement
of *employees* to refuse to handle goods where "an object thereof
is . . . forcing" the secondary employer to cease doing business
with any other person.

---

[13] Seay, *The Hot Cargo Agreement in Labor-Management Contracts,* 21
Sw. L.J. 779, 785 (1967).

[14] 357 U.S. 93, 100.

LANDRUM-GRIFFIN AND SECTION 8(e)

In 1959, Congress declared a new policy. The Landrum-Griffin Amendments to the National Labor Relations Act were intended to close many of the loopholes that had developed in regard to secondary boycotts. The 1959 amendments paid particular attention to the hot-cargo problem. Under the new law, Congress declared hot-cargo provisions unenforceable and void with a new section 8(e) which states:

> (e) It shall be an unfair labor practice for any labor organization and any employer to enter into any contract or agreement, express or implied, whereby such employer ceases or refrains or agrees to cease or refrain from handling, using, selling, transporting, or otherwise dealing in any of the products of any other employer, or to cease doing business with any other person, and any contract or agreement entered into heretofore or hereafter containing such an agreement shall be to such extent unenforcable and void: *Provided,* That nothing in this subsection (e) shall apply to an agreement between a labor organization and an employer in the construction industry relating to the contracting or subcontracting of work to be done at the site of the construction, alteration, painting, or repair of a building, structure, or other work: *Provided further,* That for the purposes of this subsection (e) and section 8(b)(4)(B) the terms "any employer," "any person engaged in commerce or an industry affecting commerce," and "any person," when used in relation to the terms "any other producer, processor, or manufacturer," "any other employer," or "any other person" shall not include persons in the relation of a jobber, manufacturer, contractor, or subcontractor working on the goods or premises of the jobber or manufacturer or performing parts of an integrated process of production in the apparel and clothing industry: Provided further, That nothing in this Act shall prohibit the enforcement of any agreement which is within the foregoing exception.[15]

In addition, the secondary boycott provisions, now designated as section 8(b)(4)(B), were changed in a manner that was intended to increase the effectiveness of the ban on secondary boycotts.[16]

---

[15] Labor-Management Reporting and Disclosure Act (Landrum-Griffin Act), § 8(e), 29 U.S.C. § 158(e) (1964).

[16] 29 U.S.C. § 158(b) (1964) now reads as follows:

It shall be an unfair labor practice for a labor organization or its agents—

. . .

(4)(i) to engage in, or to induce or encourage any individual employed by any person engaged in commerce or in an industry affecting commerce

Despite the clear language of the hot-cargo section and the plain intent of the legislative history to ban such provisions, these clauses continued to appear. Such clauses commonly dealt (1) with the right of employees of secondary employers to refuse to handle struck or nonunion goods, (2) with employee refusals to cross or work behind picket lines, and (3) with the subjects of subcontracting and work allocation. The remainder of this chapter examines the scope of section 8(e) in regard to each of these different types of provisions. Additionally, the case law shall be examined in light of the underlying policy of the Act in regard to hot-cargo provisions.

> The legislative history rather clearly shows that the Congress was intent upon banning the entry into such contracts, thereby freeing the employer from such pressures and coercion as a union might exert to obtain contractual assent to prospective secondary boycotts.[17]

Struck Work and Nonunion Goods Clauses

No substantial conflict between Board and courts exists in relation to struck and nonunion goods clauses. The rule of section 8(e) has been consistently applied. Struck work and nonunion goods clauses typically provide that the contracting employer shall not do business with a nonunion or a struck employer. In the event that the employer continues to do business with a struck or a nonunion employer, the clause permits his employees to refuse to handle such goods.

------

to engage in, a strike or a refusal in the course of his employment to use manufacture, process, transport, or otherwise handle or work on any goods, articles, materials, or commodities or to perform any services; or (ii) to threaten, coerce, or restrain any person engaged in commerce or in an industry affecting commerce, where in either case an object thereof is—

. . .

(B) forcing or requiring any person to cease using, selling, handling, transporting, or otherwise dealing in the products of any other producer, processor, or manufacturer, or to cease doing business with any other person, or forcing or requiring any other employer to recognize or bargain with a labor organization as the representative of his employees unless such labor organization has been certified as the representative of such employees under the provisions of section 159 of this title: *Provided,* That nothing contained in this clause (B) shall be construed to make unlawful, where not otherwise unlawful, any primary strike or primary picketing; . . .

[17] Teamsters Local 210 (American Feed Co.), 133 N.L.R.B. 214, 216 (1961).

In the *Lithographers Local 78 (Employing Lithographers of Greater Miami)* case [18] the Board stated the general rule governing struck work clauses. In referring to two contract provisions which the Board read as together constituting a struck work clause, the Board held that

> We read the two clauses . . . as embodying nothing more than the Board—and court—sanctioned "ally" doctrine which Congress clearly intended to preserve. As so construed, the "struck work" paragraph is lawful.[19]

Therefore, the struck work clause should embody only the "ally" doctrine.[20] It is in violation of section 8(e) to the extent that it exceeds the "ally" rules. This general rule has been affirmed in several other cases by the NLRB and courts.[21]

The rules regarding nonunion work are equally clear and there has been little difficulty in applying them to specific factual situations.

> When a clause reads that contract terms have been negotiated on the assumption that all work will be done under union conditions, and that in the event an employer requests an employee to handle work done in a nonunion shop, the Union will have the right to reopen and terminate the contract, and further contains regulations as to the use of the union label on all products, the effect is precisely the same as if the employer had agreed in so many words that he would not handle nonunion products, which is prohibited by Section 8(e). . . . So far as the employer is concerned he would be subjected to the same sanction whether he expressly "agreed" not to handle nonunion work, or whether he submitted to the language in the proposed "trade shop" clause.[22]

The above language refers to a trade shop clause, but nonunion work clauses have taken a number of different forms including trade shop, chain shop, refusal to handle, reopen, termination, and hazardous work clauses. No matter what form these clauses may

---

[18] 130 N.L.R.B. 968 (1961), *order modified*, 301 F.2d 20 (5th Cir. 1962).

[19] 130 N.L.R.B. at 974.

[20] See Chapter 4 of this study.

[21] *See* Lithographers Local 17 (Graphic Arts Employers Ass'n), 130 N.L.R.B. 985 (1961), *enforced*, 309 F.2d 31 (9th Cir. 1962); Teamsters Local 413 (Patton Warehouse, Inc.), 140 N.L.R.B. 1474 (1963), *enforced in part*, 334 F.2d 539 (D.C. Cir. 1964).

[22] 130 N.L.R.B. 968, 976.

take, the Board and courts have held all such clauses invalid where the effect is an agreement to cease doing business with another employer.[23]

> Probably no language can be explicit enough to reach in advance every possible subterfuge of resourceful parties. Nevertheless, we believe that in using the term "implied" in Section 8(e), Congress meant to reach every device which, fairly considered, is tantamount to an agreement that the contracting employer will not handle the products of another employer or cease doing business with another person.[24]

The law regarding struck goods and nonunion goods clauses is that provisions of this type are forbidden under section 8(e), unless their terms embody no more than the permissible exception embodied in the "ally" doctrine. However, as noted in an earlier chapter, the ally doctrine is a judicially created exception to the proscription on secondary boycotts. The same considerations exist in its application to hot-cargo contracts; too much discretion in the hands of the Board and the courts can lead to results that support union interests to the detriment of the interests of neutral employers, employees, and the public.

Picket Line Clauses

The case law regarding picket line clauses, which allow employees to refuse to cross or work behind picket lines, is not quite as settled as is the law with regard to nonunion and struck work clauses. The picket line clause presents the issue of whether the activity is primary and to be protected, or secondary and unenforceable and unlawful under section 8(e).

The most thorough insight into the problems presented by picket line clauses can be gained from examination of *Teamsters Local 728 (Brown Transport Corp.)*[25] and from examination of *Team-*

---

[23] *See* Lithographers Local 78 (Employing Lithographers of Greater Miami), 130 N.L.R.B. 968 (1961), *order modified*, 301 F.2d 20 (5th Cir. 1962); Lithographers Local 17 (Graphic Arts Employers Ass'n), 130 N.L.R.B. 985 (1961), *enforced*, 309 F.2d 31 (9th Cir. 1962); Teamsters Local 728 (Brown Transp. Corp.), 140 N.L.R.B. 1436 (1963), *enforced in part*, 334 F.2d 539 (D.C. Cir. 1964); Teamsters Local 413 (Patton Warehouse, Inc.), 140 N.L.R.B. 1474 (1963), *enforced in part*, 334 F.2d 539 (D.C. Cir. 1964).

[24] 130 N.L.R.B. 968, 976.

[25] 140 N.L.R.B. 1436 (1963), *enforced in part*, 334 F.2d 539 (D.C. Cir. 1964).

sters Local 413 (Patton Warehouse, Inc.).[26] The Board heard these cases separately and they were consolidated by the District of Columbia Circuit Court of Appeals. The contract clauses involved in these cases were identical. The legal issue presented by these cases was how to accomodate the terms of section 8(e) with the terms of the proviso of section 8(b) that protects primary activity.

The Board ruled in *Patton Warehouse* that

> Sections of the Act should be interpreted, so far as possible, in harmony with each other so as to effectuate the total statutory scheme. In view of the legislative concern that certain so-called secondary activities were not to be proscribed, we conclude that a "picket line" clause, whose effect may be to cause a cessation of business between two employers, is nevertheless valid under Section 8(e) insofar as it is in conformity with the proviso to Section 8(b).[27]

In effect, this holding meant that a picket line clause which prohibits employers from disciplining their employees for their refusal to cross or work behind a picket line would be valid under certain circumstances even in view of the ban contained in section 8(e). The Board held that such a clause would be valid if it were limited to those activities protected under the Act and directed against their own employer. Also the clause would be valid in regard to picketing activities by employees directed against another employer who had been struck by his own employees and where the strike had been approved by a "representative whom the employer is required to recognize under the Act."[28]

The District of Columbia Court agreed with this reasoning but modified the NLRB decision and extended the rationale beyond the proviso of section 8(b). The court held that the legislative history[29] of the amended Act and prior case law[30] clearly exhibit that the section on hot-cargo contracts was intended to apply only to

---

[26] 140 N.L.R.B. 1474 (1963), *enforced in part*, 334 F.2d 539 (D.C. Cir. 1964).

[27] 140 N.L.R.B. 1474, 1481.

[28] *Id.*

[29] 1 Legislative History of the Labor-Management Reporting and Disclosure Act of 1959 at 779 (1959). "It is settled law that the Nat. Lab. Rel. Act does not require a truck driver to cross a primary picket line . . . . [T]he employer could agree that he would not require the driver to enter the stikebound plant." *See also to same effect* 2 *id.* at 1432-33 (1959).

[30] *See* NLRB v. Rockaway News Supply Co., 345 U.S. 71 (1953).

secondary conduct and that a refusal to cross a primary picket line is protected primary activity regardless of the proviso to section 8(b). Therefore, the court decision established that picket line clauses were valid at the premises of the contracting employer:

> [T]he clause may permissibly operate to protect refusals to cross a picket line where the line is in connection with a primary dispute at the contracting employer's own premises.[31]

At the premises of another employer:

> [T]he clause may validly protect refusals to cross a picket line at the premises of *another* employer if that picket line meets the conditions expressed in the *proviso* to § 8(b)(4) of the Act.[32]

The section 8(b)(4) proviso is only applicable to refusals to enter the premises of another employer "if the employees of such employer are engaged in a strike ratified or approved by a representative of such employees whom such employer is required to recognize under this Act." These holdings are in conformity with the NLRB ruling. But the court modified the Board position in regard to refusals to cross a picket line at another employer's premises where that strike does not conform to the conditions of the section 8(b) proviso.

The court held that, at the premises of another employer, the picket line clause may validly protect refusals to cross any picket line if that picket line is primary. Such clauses cannot, however, protect an employee's refusal to cross an illegal secondary picket line.[33]

In the case of *Teamsters Local 695 (Madison Employers' Council)*,[34] the Board apparently adopted the position taken by the District of Columbia Appeals Court when it held a picket line clause invalid because it covered, "unlawful, albeit 'authorized' secondary activity."[35] On review, the District of Columbia Court agreed with this decision.

---

[31] 334 F.2d 539, 542-3.

[32] *Id.* at 543.

[33] *Id.* at 545.

[34] 152 N.L.R.B. 577 (1965), *enforced,* 361 F.2d 547 (D.C. Cir. 1966).

[35] 152 N.L.R.B. at 581.

The effect of section 8(e) upon struck and nonunion goods clauses and picket line clauses has been thorough and equitable. The decisions of the NLRB and the courts are in line with the intent of Congress to ban such clauses as undesirable contracts to engage in secondary boycotts. At the same time, the Board and the courts have sought to protect the interests of unions to engage in primary activity. Struck and nonunion goods clauses may encompass but may not surpass the dictates of the "ally" doctrine. Primary picket lines may be the subject of contract clauses allowing employees to refuse to cross. The underlying policy of the secondary boycott provisions is maintained by these rules. The interests of neutral employers are protected from undue interference and the rights of unions to engage in primary activity are maintained.

SUBCONTRACTING AND WORK ALLOCATION

The application and interpretation of section 8(e) proved to be a much more difficult task in regard to subcontracting and work allocation clauses. The resulting controversy primarily involved the NLRB and the District of Columbia Circuit Court of Appeals. Both the Board and the court agreed that a subcontracting clause could not limit subcontracting work to union firms only. On the other hand, clauses which precluded all subcontracting to anyone at all were valid. The conflict that developed between the NLRB views and those of the District of Columbia Court involved the determination of whether these latter agreements constituted a promise to subcontract to union firms only.

Union Signatory and Union Standard Clauses

In early cases involving subcontracting and work preservation the NLRB and District of Columbia Court agreed that valid economic considerations support such restrictive clauses, but that when these clauses exceed allowable bounds the potential for harm greatly increases. In the *Machinists District 9 (Greater St. Louis Automotive Association)* case,[36] the Board, with subsequent court agreement, distinguished between valid and invalid work allocation clauses.

> The contract clause which prohibits, limits, or restricts subcontracting of work ordinarily performed by employees in the unit covered by the contract is fairly common in modern collective-bargaining

---

[36] 134 N.L.R.B. 1354 (1961), *enforced*, 315 F.2d 33 (D.C. Cir. 1962).

agreements. Generally, the purpose and object of such restrictions is to preserve the jobs and job rights of the employees in the unit covered by the contract. We do not in this case decide whether such contract clauses are lawful or unlawful. However, article XXIX is more than a restriction on subcontracting for the preservation of jobs and job rights of employees. Article XXIX *allows* subcontracting of work ordinarily performed by employees covered by the contract. It limits the persons *with whom* the employer can do business. We see no meaningful distinction between a contract which prohibits an employer from handling products produced by a nonunion firm and a contract which causes an employer to cease subcontracting work to a nonunion firm. Both clearly violate Section 8(e).[37]

The Board and courts have therefore taken the position that all subcontracting and work allocation clauses appear at first to violate section 8. But the Board and the courts have found important considerations present which have enabled them to draw distinctions between lawful subcontracting clauses, which have as their object the protection and preservation of unit work, and unlawful clauses, which only forbid subcontracting to nonunion subcontractors. The District of Columbia Court stated that subcontracting clauses are permitted because through them, "the union is seeking to protect some legitimate economic interest of the employees. . ., and not just using its position . . . to enforce its demands against subcontractors."[38]

In allowing even these "legitimate" subcontracting clauses, the Board and the courts ignore many valid economic interests of subcontractors and other secondary employers and employees. These interests and not those of unit employees are the subject of section 8(e). It is not clear that the interests of unit employees outweigh the interests of secondary parties. The initial Board position, that clauses which limit the persons with whom the employer can do business violated section 8(e), achieved a balance between these interests. The balance should not be upset by finding new factors to use as a means of removing situations from the coverage of section 8(e). However, the District of Columbia Court did just this when it created the union signatory-union standards distinction.

---

[37] 134 N.L.R.B. at 1358.

[38] Bakery Wagon Drivers and Salesmen Local 484 v. N.L.R.B., 321 F.2d 353, 358 (D.C. Cir. 1963).

In *Orange Belt District Council of Painters No. 48 v. NLRB*,[39] the District of Columbia Court stated its test for determining the validity of subcontracting clauses.

> The key question presented by subcontracting clauses in union agreements with general contractors is whether they are addressed to the labor relations of the subcontractor, rather than the general contractor. . . . The test as to the "primary" nature of a subcontracting clause in an agreement with a general contractor has been phrased by scholars as whether it "will directly benefit employees covered thereby" and "seeks to protect the wages and job opportunities of the employees covered by the contract." We have phrased the test as whether the clauses are "germane to the economic integrity of the principal work unit" and seek "to protect and preserve the work and standards (the union) has bargained for" or instead "extend beyond the (contracting) employer" and are aimed really at the union's difference with another employer.[40]

The phrasing of the court's test has some support in the statute and its legislative history. Section 8(e) is intended to void all agreements which amount to secondary boycotts. The above test merely states a useful means of differentiating primary and secondary activity. This is not the exclusive determinant of the validity of such clauses and it cannot be applied too broadly.

The subcontracting issues presented in *Patton Warehouse* serve as a useful means of examining the NLRB and the District of Columbia Circuit Court views. The NLRB found that the clause violated section 8(e). The subcontracting clause required that the employer refrain from subcontracting to any person who did not observe the wages, hours, and other working conditions that prevailed in unions having jurisdiction over the same type of work. The NLRB ruled that this clause established requirements to govern with whom the employer should be allowed to do business. The Board ruled that the clause was not concerned with the protection or preservation of unit work since subcontracting was allowed under the established circumstances.

The District of Columbia Court, relying on its past decisions, ruled that the contract clause in the *Patton* case was not void and was not prohibited by section 8(e). The court criticized the NLRB decision for failing to distinguish between "contract clauses which impose boycotts on subcontractors not signatory to union agreements, and those which merely require subcontractors to meet the

---

[39] 328 F.2d 534 (D.C. Cir. 1964).

[40] *Id.* at 538.

equivalent of a union standard in order to protect the work of the employees of the contracting employer." [41] The court continued by holding that this was the vital distinction upon which the determination of the legality of the clause is made. The court established the rule that, "Union-signatory subcontracting clauses are secondary, and therefore within the scope of § 8(e), while union-standards subcontracting clauses are primary as to the contracting employer." [42]

In *Teamsters Local 710 (Wilson & Co.)*[43] the NLRB and the court each took their respective positions on subcontracting clauses and section 8(e). However, the NLRB decision was rendered by a closely divided Board. Chairman McCulloch stated that in dealing with subcontracting clauses, it is foreseeable that there will arise,

> . . . circumstances in which contract provisions relating to wages or working conditions under which subcontracting may be allowed are so clearly and directly related to the protection of the unit employees' work that they are permissible under the statute, as being "strictly germane to the economic integrity of the principal work unit." [44]

The narrow majority that upheld the NLRB position in *Wilson* (that subcontracting clauses are illegal where they dictate with whom the employer may or may not subcontract) grew even weaker. By 1966 the Board view had changed completely.

In *Teamsters Local 107 (S & E McCormick, Inc.)*[45] the NLRB reversed its own position and adopted the position taken by the D.C. Circuit in *Orange Belt, Patton,* and *Wilson.* The contract clause involved in *McCormick* read as follows:

ARTICLE 33
SUBCONTRACTING

(a) The Employer agrees to refrain from using the sevrices of any person who does not observe the wages, hours, and conditions of

---

[41] 334 F.2d 539, 548.

[42] *Id.*

[43] 143 N.L.R.B. 1221 (1963), *enforced in part, set aside in part, remanded in part,* 335 F.2d 709 (D.C. Cir. 1964).

[44] 143 N.L.R.B. at 1239.

[45] 159 N.L.R.B. 84 (1966), *vacated and remanded on other grounds sub. nom.* A. Duie Pyle, Inc. v. N.L.R.B., 383 F.2d 772 (D.C. Cir. 1967).

employment established by labor unions having jurisdiction over the type of services performed.[46]

This clause is identical to one found illegal under section 8(e) in the Board's *Patton* decision. The Board reviewed its own reasoning in *Patton* and that of the Circuit Court.

> We have since reconsidered our decision in light of the court's reasoning and we now conclude in agreement with the court that the clause is primary, and thus not violative of Section 8(e).[47]

This one area concerning secondary boycotts, like so many of the other boycott situations, has witnessed a gradual watering down of the statutory proscription in favor of union interests. The 1959 Amendments were specifically intended to ban all secondary boycott hot-cargo contracts. The District of Columbia Court led the Board to create new and artificial distinctions that partially defeat the intent of the law. The philosophy underlying the D.C. Court's signatory-standards distinction was to have an even wider influence on all hot-cargo situations.

The Work-Preservation Doctrine

The single most important case dealing with hot-cargo agreements since the Landrum-Griffin Amendments is *Brotherhood of Carpenters and Joiners (National Woodwork Manufacturers Association).*[48] This case established the work-preservation doctrine as the main criterion for determining the legality or illegality of activity under section 8(e).

The facts of this case were not unique. The general contractor at a construction project was a party to a collective bargaining contract which forbade union members from handling pre-machined doors. The contracting employer ignored this provision and ordered pre-cut doors which his employees refused to handle. These doors were then replaced by blanks. The seller of the pre-cut doors was a member of the National Woodwork Manufacturers Association which charged that the union contract "will not handle" provision violated section 8(e).

---

[46] 159 N.L.R.B. at 93.

[47] *Id.* at 102.

[48] 149 N.L.R.B. 646 (1964), *rev'd in part*, 354 F.2d 594 (7th Cir. 1965), *rev'd in part*, 386 U.S. 612 (1967). *See also* Houston Insulation Contractors Ass'n v. N.L.R.B., 386 U.S. 664 (1967).

The NLRB affirmed the Trial Examiner's ruling that the contract provision was valid. The NLRB held that the clause in question had work preservation as its object and the enforcement of such a clause against the general contractor was primary. The Seventh Circuit Court of Appeals reversed and held that the clause and its enforcement were illegal under section 8(e). The Supreme Court disagreed with the Seventh Circuit Court and adopted the work preservation rationale.

The Supreme Court decision began by tracing the history of union unfair labor practices for secondary boycotts. It stated that the passage of section 8(e) was for the purpose of closing loopholes opened by its last hot-cargo decision, *Sand Door*.

> The *Sand Door* decision was believed by Congress not only to create the possibility of damage actions against employers for breaches of "hot cargo" clauses, but also to create a situation in which such clauses might be employed to exert subtle pressures upon employers to engage in "voluntary" boycotts.[49]

From this point, the Court indulged in a tortuous analysis of the legislative history of the amended Act and arrived at the conclusion that section 8(e) should not encompass employees' primary activity; and that the section does not ban employees' agreements made to pressure a primary employer for purposes of protecting and preserving work traditionally done by them. The scope and reach of section 8(e) was tied by the Court to section 8(b)(4)(B) and its primary activity proviso. In speaking of section 8(e) and its function, the Court stated:

> This loophole-closing measure likewise did not expand the type of conduct which [the original] § 8(b)(4)(A) condemned. Although the language of Section 8(e) is sweeping, it closely tracks that of § 8(b)(4)(A), and just as the latter and its successor § 8(b)(4)(B) did not reach employees' activity to pressure their employer to preserve for themselves work traditionally done by them, § 8(e) does not prohibit agreements made and maintained for that purpose.[50]

The Supreme Court also found strong confirmation in the construction and garment industries' exemptions that Congress intended both sections 8(e) and 8(b)(4)(B) to reach only secondary activity. The Court finally resorted to the decision in *Fibreboard*

---

[49] 386 U.S. 612, 634.

[50] *Id.* at 635.

Paper Products Corp. v. NLRB,[51] a case which dealt with section 8(a)(5), as having implicitly recognized the legitimacy of work preservation clauses. But section 8(a)(5) and the *Fibreboard* case deal with the duty to bargain over the terms and conditions of employment. This is clearly distinguishable and has no application to hot-cargo secondary boycott cases.

The Court's reasoning is protracted and strained. After having sidestepped the clear language of the statute and its underlying policy and having created a new policy, the Court enunciated its rule, that the validity of a "will not handle" clause and its enforcement under section 8(e) and section 8(b)(4)(B) depends upon

> . . . whether, under all the surrounding circumstances, the Union's objective was preservation of work for Frouge's employees, or whether the agreements and boycott were tactically calculated to satisfy union objectives elsewhere. Were the latter the case, Frouge, the boycotting employer, would be a neutral bystander, and the agreement or boycott would, within the intent of Congress, become secondary. There need not be an actual dispute with the boycotted employer . . . for the activity to fall within this category, so long as the tactical object of the agreement and its maintenance is that employer, or benefits to other than the boycotting employees or other employees of the primary employer thus making the agreement or boycott secondary in its aim. The touchstone is whether the agreement or its maintenance is addressed to the labor relations of the contracting employer *vis-a-vis* his own employees.[52]

In a strong dissenting opinion, Mr. Justice Stewart joined by Justices Black, Douglas, and Clark, stated that the boycott and the contract clause here involved fall clearly within the prohibition of the Act.

> The Court undertakes a protracted review of legislative and decisional history in an effort to show that the clear words of the statute should be disregarded in these cases. . . . The Court overlooks the fact that a product boycott for work preservation purposes has consistently been regarded by the courts, and by the Congress that passed the Taft-Hartley Act, as a proscribed "secondary boycott." [53]

---

[51] 379 U.S. 203 (1964). *See also* Rabin, *Fibreboard and the Termination of Bargaining Unit Work*, 71 Colum. L. Rev. 803 (1971), which illustrates this point and takes exception with Board and court over-extension of the *Fibreboard* doctrine.

[52] 386 U.S. 612, 644, 645.

[53] *Id.* at 650, 652.

The dissent conducted a detailed analysis of the case law and legislative history dealing with product boycotts for work preservation. Its well supported conclusion was that the Court seemed to have substituted its own policy for the policy enacted by Congress in 1947 and strengthened by Congress in 1959.

The *National Woodwork* doctrine was a judicially framed and enforced policy. Its roots go back to the union standards and union signatory distinctions of the Distirct of Columbia Circuit Court of Appeals. The work preservation doctrine gained further support from the New Frontier NLRB. Its acceptance and promulgation by 5 to 4 majority of the Supreme Court in *National Woodwork* established the doctrine of work preservation as the major criterion for determining the validity of subcontracting and work allocation clauses.

In *Pipe Fitters Local 455 and Plumbers Local 34 (American Boiler Manufacturers Association)*[54] the work preservation doctrine was the sole criterion relied upon by the Board and by the Eighth Circuit Court in dismissing charges of a section 8(e) unfair labor practice. In *Asbestos Workers Local 8 (Preformed Metal Products Co.)*[55] a violation of section 8(e) was found to exist, but the sole criterion of determination was the doctrine from *National Woodwork*. But, as stated by Mr. Justice Stewart in his dissent in *National Woodwork*, such a test is unnecessarily restrictive and improperly narrow.

> . . . § 8(b)(4) [like § 8(e)] is not limited to boycotts that have as their only purpose the forcing of any person to cease using the products of another; it is sufficient if that result is "an object" of the boycott. Legitimate union objectives may not be accomplished through means proscribed by the statute.[56]

The work preservation doctrine does not encompass this broad outlook advocated by Mr. Justice Stewart. The Court's decision completely ignores or overrules the fundamental principal that if the boycott has as one of its objects the forcing or requiring of a cessation of business between one employer and another, then the fact that another object, such as work protection, exists is completely irrelevant.

---

[54] 167 N.L.R.B. 602 (1967), *remanded,* 404 F.2d 547 (8th Cir. 1968).

[55] 173 N.L.R.B. 330 (1968).

[56] 386 U.S. 612, 651.

The effect of the work preservation doctrine is to weaken the statutory ban on secondary boycott contract clauses. As a policy created by the judiciary, its scope and application should, at the very least, be restricted to the same type of cases from which it arose. This has not been the case.

Right to Control

The right to control test has historically been utilized by the NLRB and the Courts to determine the status of an employer with regard to a particular dispute involving work allocation. Essentially, the test required that the employer have the right to control the matter at issue in order to be designated a primary employer. Where such right to control has not been present, the employer's status has been that of a neutral or secondary employer.

The *International Longshoremen's Association (Board of Harbor Commissioners)* case [57] provides a good example of the effect of "right to control" prior to *National Woodwork*. The Board's decision in *Harbor Commissioners* stated that

> The Board has held, with court approval, that where the employer, under economic pressure by a union is without power to resolve the underlying dispute, such employer is the secondary or neutral employer and that the employer with power to resolve the dispute is the primary employer.[58]

The Third Circuit Court of Appeals affirmed this reasoning in *Harbor Commissioners*. It has also been adopted by the Sixth Circuit Court of Appeals.[59]

The typical situation under which the right to control test has been applied by the Board and courts has involved a subcontracting situation. An employer who has agreed to a valid subcontracting or work allocation provision in his contract with the union is required by the general contractor to take some action that would violate the collective bargaining control provision but which is also quite consistent with the terms of the subcontracting arrangement. For such situations the NLRB and the courts have determined that since the subcontractor employer lacks the right to resolve the dispute, he is to be regarded as a secondary employer to

---

[57] 137 N.L.R.B. 1178 (1962), *enforced*, 331 F.2d 712 (3rd Cir. 1964).

[58] 137 N.L.R.B. at 1182.

[59] *See* Ohio Valley Carpenters District Council (Cardinal Industries), 144 N.L.R.B. 91 (1963), *enforced*, 339 F.2d 142 (6th Cir. 1964).

that dispute. This result does not leave the union without a means of satisfying its demands. In this situation the general contractor has been regarded as the primary employer and economic pressure may be exerted by the union upon him.

The *National Woodwork* case did not ostensibly change the legal status of the right to control standard. The NLRB and the Seventh Circuit relied on the right to control test in their decisions. The Supreme Court expressly declared that their decision was not to bear upon the right to control issue. Nevertheless, since *National Woodwork*, several court decisions have rejected the test in whole or in part.

The Third Circuit Court of Appeals, which had adopted the right to control test in the *Harbor Commissioners* case, ruled that the right to control is only one factor to be considered in determining the legality of the union objective. This decision was reached in the *International Brotherhool of Electrical Workers Local 164 (Ridgewood Board of Education)* case [60] in which the court also indicated that where the dispute concerns work preservation solely and the union's attempts to enforce the work preservation clause against the contracting employer, there would be no violation of section 8. Similar results have been reached by the Eighth [61] and the First Circuits.[62]

Most recently the NLRB view was completely rejected by the District of Columbia Circuit Court in the *Plumbing and Pipefitting Local 636 (Mechanical Contractors Association of Detroit) v. NLRB* case.[63] The Court held that the right to control test as a means of distinguishing between primary and secondary union activity was a mechanical and artificial rule that ignores the realities of the dispute and relies solely on whether the employer is capable of settling the dispute. Relying on the rationale expressed in *National Woodwork*, the Court remanded the case to the Board with instructions to make a finding consistent with the Court's opinion.

---

[60] 158 N.L.R.B. 838 (1966), *enforcement denied*, 388 F.2d 105 (3rd Cir. 1968).

[61] *See* American Boiler Manufacturers Ass'n v. N.L.R.B., 404 F.2d 556 (8th Cir. 1968).

[62] *See* Beacon Castle Square Bldg. Corp. v. N.L.R.B., 406 F.2d 188 (1st Cir. 1969).

[63] 430 F.2d 906 (D.C. Cir. 1970).

On remand, the NLRB [64] acquiesced to the view of the D.C. Court and found that *for the purposes of this case only,* the right to control test would be abandoned and dismissed the case.

In *Carpenters Local 742 (J. L. Simmons Co.)*,[65] the most recent right to control case, the NLRB and the District of Columbia Court reaffirmed their respective, conflicting positions. Subsequently, the Supreme Court declined to review [66] the lower court's decision, lending some strength to the position that the NLRB must abandon the right to control test as a per se rule in product boycott cases. The effect of the Court's decision is to require that the "right to control" test no longer be relied upon as the *sole* basis for finding an unlawful product boycott.

Even though the Supreme Court has refused to review this question and the NLRB has acquiesed to the view of the District of Columbia Court in the *Mechanical Contractors Association of Detroit* and in the *J. L. Simmons* cases, the Board has given no indication that it will abandon the right to control test. The Board has not been bound by court of appeals decisions which disagree with its view. Only in the event of a Supreme Court decision would the Board be bound to follow a different ruling.

Stable and predictable industrial relations demand that a Supreme Court decision on the right to control issue be made soon, for it has been severely weakened by the circuit courts' repudiation. The right to control test has proved its value as an analytical tool in solving the primary-secondary dichotomy. The present controversy is the result of the application of the work preservation doctrine, a rule created by the judiciary, to an area of the law where it has no place. Before the union objective enters the picture, the status of the parties must be ascertained and ascertainable. "Right to control" makes this determination ascertainable. Moreover, it is a simple test, easily understood and easily applied. By weakening the right to control test and by relying on the work preservation theories that arose in *National Woodwork*, the administration of the Act is unnecessarily complicated and the true object and

---

[64] Plumbing and Pipefitting Local 636 (Mechanical Contractors Association of Detroit), 189 N.L.R.B. No. 99, 76 L.R.R.M. 1716 (1971) (complaint dismissed).

[65] 178 N.L.R.B. No. 54, 72 L.R.R.M. 1107 (1970) *enforcement denied,* .... F.2d ...., 76 L.R.R.M. 2976 (D.C. Cir. 1970).

[66] .... U.S. ...., 78 L.R.R.M. 2986 (1971).

motive of union activity is ignored. The effect of the new rules is to set aside the secondary boycott protections in the law, to by-pass the protection afforded to neutral and public interests, and to produce adverse economic consequences that highly inflate construction costs by banning premanufactured goods.

CONSTRUCTION AND GARMENT PROVISOS

Section 8(e) also contains two provisos. The first applies to the construction industry and creates a limited exception for unions and employers in the construction industry who make hot-cargo agreements concerning work done at the site of the construction. The second proviso creates an absolute exception from sections 8(e) and 8(b)(4)(B) for the apparel and clothing industry.

Construction

In the 1964 case of *Building and Construction Trades Council (Centlivre Village Apartments)*[67] the NLRB adopted its present position regarding strikes to obtain and enforce hot-cargo clauses under the provision. Prior to 1964 the NLRB had previously held that under the proviso to section 8(e), a strike to obtain or to enforce a valid hot-cargo clause was, nevertheless, illegal.[68] In *Centlivre* the Board modified its position and now ruled that strikes that were for the purpose of obtaining a hot-cargo clause were permissible under the construction proviso. However, the NLRB has continually held that strikes to enforce a valid hot-cargo clause are in violation of section 8(b)(4)(B). This change in the Board's view had the effect of once again extending the coverage of the Act in a manner that unduly favors the interests and power of unions. The NLRB's new rule creates an imbalance that is contrary to the intent of Congress and the public policy implication of sections 8(b)(4) and 8(e).

The construction proviso is specifically limited to "work to be done at the site of the construction." The NLRB has interpreted this provision to require that the work actually be done at the construction site and that there be a past history showing that the

---

[67] 148 N.L.R.B. 854 (1964), *enforcement denied*, 352 F.2d 696 (D.C. Cir. 1965).

[68] *See* Construction, Production, and Maintenance Laborers Local 383 (Colson & Stevens Construction Co.), 137 N.L.R.B. 1650 (1962), *rev'd*, 323 F.2d 422 (9th Cir. 1963).

work was customarily performed on the site of the job.[69] Additionally, it has been held that in the construction industry hot-cargo clauses pertaining to jobsite work do not violate anti-trust laws because of the sanctions contained in the proviso to section 8(e).[70]

Clothing and Apparel

The second proviso grants an absolute exemption to the garment industry. Hot-cargo clauses in all forms are legal in the clothing and apparel industries and can be obtained or enforced by a strike. The provisions are clear and absolute. No litigation has arisen before the NLRB or the courts.

CONCLUDING REMARKS

Section 8(e) was enacted by Congress with the intent of maintaining whatever prohibitions on hot-cargo clauses already in existence and of closing the loopholes opened by the Supreme Court's *Sand Door* decision. In that case the Court had called for congressional policy changes as the only way of prohibiting certain activity.

Section 8(e) was Congress' response. For a period of several years after the passage of the new amendments, the NLRB rules followed the statutory mandate and hot-cargo clauses were banned. Even today, nonunion goods and struck work clauses are only allowable to the extent that they encompass the ally doctrine. However, in areas dealing with work allocation and subcontracting clauses, the NLRB has abandoned its original position which treats such clauses harshly and has adopted the District of Columbia Court's and Supreme Court's work preservation doctrine as the sole criterion for determining the objective of the union. The supremacy of work preservation has severely undermined the protection that the Act was intended to afford to neutral employers and to the public. The work preservation doctrine should, at most, be only one of several factors considered in determining the union object.

Furthermore, the District of Columbia Court has attempted to abolish the right to control test and replace it with new standards that are consistent with the work preservation doctrine. The pri-

---

[69] *See* Ohio Valley Carpenters District Council (Cardinal Industries), 136 N.L.R.B. 977 (1962).

[70] See Connell Construction Company, Inc. and United Association Local 100, U.S. D.C., N. Dist. Tex., Civil Action 3-4455-B, November 16, 1971.

mary-secondary dichotomy is not to be solved by inquiries that look to the objective of the union. The right to control is an essential factor in determining the status of an employer and in protecting neutrals.

Overall, the passage of section 8(e) has not closed loopholes as Congress envisioned. The case law under section 8(e) has shown a strong trend to undermine gradually and even to ignore the plain language of the statute that bans hot-cargo secondary boycott contracts. By focusing on the propensity to protect and preserve unit work, the NLRB and the courts give little or no cognizance to the interests of neutral employers, inhibit the use and development of new technology, and overlook the public interest that generated the legislation.

The powerful "work preservation" doctrine of the NLRB and the courts has created a critical situation. Work preservation and protection has enabled unions in some cases completely to forestall the use of more economical and advanced techniques. This situation has assumed critical proportions in the construction, printing, and food retailing industries.[71] The current position of the NLRB, as can be seen in the case law, is that even though the clear intention of the unions is to conduct strikes or picketing that disturbs or halts existing or future business dealings, such activity is not proscribed by sections 8(b)(4) or 8(e) where the unions may be attributed with an object of preserving the work of the bargaining unit.

The current NLRB rules are contrary to public policy as envisioned by Congress and as embodied in section 8(e). The work preservation doctrine as enunciated by the Supreme Court and as extended by the Board and the D.C. Circuit Court enables unions to use the product boycott as a means of imposing the conditions under which work is to be performed and to require uneconomic restrictions in the planning and conduct of business. Work preservation has enabled unions to ban prefabricated materials and other innovative and economical techniques from the construction job

---

[71] The long history of restrictive labor practices in the construction industry is a matter of common knowledge. Although not as well known, the printing industry unions have also succeeded effectively in slowing technological advances, particularly in the newspaper industry. The New York newspaper negotiations of the last decade provide an excellent case study of this problem and the demise of daily papers there. Finally, see H. Northrup, Restrictive Labor Practices in the Supermarket Industry (1967). This study provides an authoritative analysis of all restrictive practices in the retail food industry and provides valuable insights that apply equally well to construction and printing.

site. The effect of these boycotts extends far beyond the primary parties. By raising the costs of conducting business in such diverse industries as construction, printing, and food retailing, the public interest is severely and adversely affected.

CHAPTER VI

Conclusion

It seems clear from this review of cases that the NLRB and the courts have failed to carry out the statutory ban on secondary boycotts to the degree envisioned by Congress. In each area here examined, a general trend exists. During the first few years of the sixties, the Act was applied in a manner that was most consistent with the legislative history and the clear provisions of the Act. Since that time, however, there has been a gradual weakening of the prohibition on secondary boycotts. Instead of closing the loopholes that existed in 1959, the case law reveals that new loopholes have arisen to replace the old. The net effect is that the secondary boycott remains a key weapon in the union arsenal.

Allowing unions to maintain powerful weapons to resolve labor conflicts with employers is desirable. It is a cornerstone of our national labor policy to maintain an equality of bargaining power. It is only when these powers become too great that an undesirable imbalance results. Such an imbalance has existed and continues to exist in regard to secondary boycotts. Congress recognized the boycott as being counterproductive and took corrective measures in 1947 and again in 1959. Nevertheless, in 1972 this imbalance continues.

The secondary boycott not only adversely affects the primary employer as is its intent, but it also extends the dispute to neutral secondary employers and their employees and to the public. It is this extension that makes the secondary boycott undesirable.

The approach of the NLRB and of the courts has been to attempt to distinguish between boycotts that are primary, even though there are secondary effects, and those that are secondary. The byproduct of this approach is the current imbalance on the side of union interests to the detriment of those of the secondary employer, his employees, and the public. Perhaps the real fallacy exists not in the distinctions as drawn by the NLRB but in the attempt to draw such fine lined distinctions at all. If it is not possible to draw such distinctions in a manner that provides balanced protection of the interests of unions and those of all neutral parties, including the public, then the only solution remaining is to ban all secondary boycotts. Such a course provides adequate protection to neutrals and does not at all undermine the strength of unions. Under today's conditions, the removal of this one union tool does not affect union power to a substantial degree. It only prevents labor disputes from being extended beyond the primary parties in a manner that is detrimental to neutral parties and that is counterproductive to the flow of commerce. The essential ingredient in any solution is to balance the respective interests involved. Such balance would permit unions to engage in primary activity and at the same time allow secondary parties and the public to avoid becoming enmeshed in labor disputes with the detrimental and undesirable consequences of such involvement.

Index of Cases